Rough and Rowdy Ways

Number Four
TARLETON STATE UNIVERSITY
SOUTHWESTERN STUDIES IN THE HUMANITIES
William T. Pilkington, Series Editor

ROUGH AND ROWDY WAYS

The Life and Hard Times
of Edward Anderson

BY PATRICK BENNETT

TEXAS A&M UNIVERSITY PRESS
COLLEGE STATION

"My Rough and Rowdy Ways," copyright 1931 by Southern Music Publishing Co., Inc. Words by Elsie MacWilliams, music by Jimmie Rodgers

Frontispiece: Pencil portrait of Edward by Karl Sherman

The paper used in this book meets the minimum requirements of the American National Standard for Permanence of Paper for Printed Library Materials, Z39.48-1984. Binding materials have been chosen for durability.

Library of Congress Cataloging-in-Publication Data

Bennett, Patrick, 1931–
   Rough and rowdy ways : the life and hard times of Edward Anderson
   by Patrick Bennett.
      p. cm.—(Tarleton State University southwestern studies in the humanities ; no. 4)
   Bibliography: p.
   Includes index.
   ISBN 0-89096-352-5 :
   1. Anderson, Edward, 1905–1969. 2. Authors, American—20th
century—Biography. I. Title.
PS3501.N218Z587 1988
813'.52—dc19
[B]   88-11151
                                           CIP

For Patrick C. and David,
and the children of Edward:
    I hope you will try hard
      to understand your parents,
      as hard as I have tried
      to understand my own.

But somehow I can't forget
My good old rambling days;
The railroad trains are calling me always;
I may be rough, I may be wild,
I may be tough and counted vile,
But I can't give up
My good old rough and rowdy ways.

—old Jimmie Rodgers song

Contents

Illustrations

Preface

During the Great Depression a young man named Edward Anderson, who had learned to sculpt a sentence while working on newspapers in Oklahoma and Texas, turned to serious writing. His fiction soon earned high praise on both sides of the Atlantic. This book is mostly about his career in the 1930s and 1940s, when he was writing short stories, novels, radio plays, and screenplays. I have also touched on his formative years and his later life, but my story centers on his two middle decades, his most productive years.

His career gives us insight into the literary world of the thirties. Anderson's victories and defeats tell us much about what a talented young writer from the Southwest could achieve by writing "poor-folks fiction," a genre that fascinated critics during those hard times. To understand an era, we must examine the individuals who lived through it. Page Smith, in his book *Dissenting Opinions,* says that "Without the feeling of real lives, deeply lived, there can be no real history, whatever you may call it. Without the sense of lives lived, the inherent drama of history is lost: no drama, no history."

To trace Anderson's life, I have relied heavily on the memories of his family, of his friends, of friends of his friends. I unearthed some documents, but during his productive years Anderson kept no journal and wrote few letters. Both memories and documents are imperfect sources. Making a narrative from documents alone is often like making a portrait of primitive man on the basis of a tooth, a shinbone, and a flint scraper. Memory, on the other hand, can be incomplete or dictated by emotions, and it sometimes juggles the sequence of events. Yet memory has the juice of life. Forced to a choice, I would take memory.

Finding out anything at all about Anderson was not easy. I first learned of this remarkable man and his two novels through a couple of sentences in A.C. Greene's *A Personal Country* when it was published in the fall of 1969. Ironically, Anderson died within a few days of *Personal Country*'s publication, though neither Greene nor I was aware of it at the time. My curiosity was aroused. A first-rate novelist who had written here in Abilene? As a young man Anderson had worked on the *Abilene Reporter-News,* but nobody had ever mentioned him during my six years on that newspaper's staff. Time passed, and I got around to reading Anderson's novels. *Hungry Men* and *Thieves Like Us* had aged beautifully; I was surprised to find them so good. My curiosity grew.

What happened to Anderson? Why did he publish only two novels? Houston writer Max Apple suggested a pair of related questions to me: Why did his novels get such immediate and favorable attention when published, and why were they neglected so soon afterwards?

Austin poet and novelist Paul Foreman was also interested in Anderson. Foreman's Thorp Spring Press had recently published a book by the late Charles Seltzer of El Paso, *The Collected Stories of Amado Muro.* Foreman learned that Seltzer had been a friend of Anderson's. Amada Seltzer, Charles's widow, said that she and her husband believed that Anderson had died in Houston in the 1960s. But I could find no record of his death there.

Before any questions could be answered, I had to find out which way from Abilene he went. Anderson left few tracks in this town, and half a century had obliterated most of those. Maureen Eastus, who had been on the *Reporter-News* staff with Anderson, suggested a search of old Abilene city directories. In them Anderson first popped up during the twenties, as a newspaper employee. By checking for other persons named Anderson at Edward's address, I learned the names of other members of his family. In Taylor County records I found that an Edward Anderson had married a Polly Anne Bates (but the newspaper had not carried a wedding story). To confuse matters, there were other Edward Andersons in the directories and records, but faint clues usually indicated which was my man. The last members of Edward Anderson's family seemed to disappear from Abilene during World War II.

Which way did they go? A half dozen trails led me to nothing. I was baffled, but Lloyd Lyman, of Texas A&M University Press, an admirer of Anderson's *Thieves Like Us,* urged me to keep looking.

Finally, an old tragedy pointed the way. E. H. Anderson, Edward's father, vanished from the city directory around 1936, and Edward's mother was listed thereafter as a widow. I found the father's obituary in the newspaper, but it was no help except in mentioning that he was buried in "a local cemetery." Sure enough, Abilene's long-established City Cemetery contained the grave of Edward's father, and a cemetery official told me in 1982 that he had recently received a letter from Edward's mother, then more than ninety years old and living in Dallas.

When I opened the Dallas telephone directory to the page listing Andersons, the door began to open a little bit on what had happened to Edward Anderson. His mother, when I rang her up, was in no mood for a long conversation, nor was she inclined to a detailed answer to the letter I subsequently sent her, but she gave me the address of Edward's daughter, Helen, in Fort Myers, Florida. So I wrote Helen.

That summer, when I got back from vacation, the college switchboard operator told me that an Anne Anderson had tried to phone me from Florida.

Excited, I dialed the number she had left.

"Hello."

"Is this the Anne Anderson who was married to Edward Anderson?"

"Three times!"

The door continued to open. The following pages show what happened to Edward Anderson.

Rough and Rowdy Ways

1. Catching up
with the Lost Generation

One day in 1930 Edward Euell Anderson looked out over the news-room of the *Houston Post*. Now that the deadline was past, the last story edited and headed and spiked, Anderson had the leisure to lean back in his chair, flex his line-gauge between his hands, and observe his fellow journalists: the managing editor talking on a phone, with the bell-shaped receiver cocked at his ear, a rimmer opening a pack of cigarettes that he was fetching back to the copy desk, other members of the staff unwinding, straightening desks, jawing. "Legalized prostitution" was the term Anderson had come to apply to the work going on in this typical newsroom. News stories: bunk, baloney, a bunch of hooey.

Anderson seemed the same dapper, clean-shaven young newspaper-man he was three months ago, or three weeks ago, but he had come to a couple of conclusions that would change his life. First, he wanted to write something more substantial than newspaper copy, maybe magazine stories, maybe hardback books. There was supposed to be a lot of money in a Literary Guild selection. Second, he wanted to begin his new career by taking a look at Europe, something many American writers had done in the 1920s. These were fateful decisions, because Anderson and the new decade were made for one another. A writer cannot choose the era of his best, most productive years any more than he can choose the color of his eyes or the length of his frame. Anderson, blue-eyed, 5'8" head to heel, would thrive in the 1930s, in the conditions of the Great Depression, the way some tropical fish thrive only among certain water plants, in water of a specific temperature.

A printer in an ink-stained apron walked among the desks in the large, open room, distributing copies of the current edition so that everyone could check for errors. Anderson glanced through the first section, happy to find that the compositor had squeezed a headline Anderson had been afraid would prove a few points too long. Then he turned to the sports section to see what, if anything, had happened in the world of boxing. Anderson had once fought professionally himself.

A fellow *Post* staff member named Melba Newton came over to talk to Anderson (whom she called "Andy"). An attractive woman, slender, 5'6", with light auburn hair and blue eyes, Melba was five years older than Andy. She was an experienced reporter and a good one. She asked him if he were ready to eat. Of course he would eat with her. They were very much in love, Andy and Melba. He had asked her to marry him, asked several times. She had turned him down. Melba wasn't ready to settle down just yet.

As they came out of the building into the night, Andy would wonder whether to tell Melba that he had decided to give his two weeks' notice. He planned to sign on as a deckhand on a ship bound for Europe. He felt sure that when he got back he could pick up another newspaper job just like that, provided he wanted it. Like most persons, Anderson could not guess that by 1930 the dance had ended for the wild, gaudy, alcoholic times called the "Jazz Age" by F. Scott Fitzgerald (a writer as uniquely suited to the 1920s as Anderson was to the 1930s). Anyway, why spoil a meal? Why not tell Melba later? Andy was a closemouthed man, seldom in a hurry to reveal his plans. There was no big rush.

Melba was his true friend of the moment. Although Anderson got along well with other persons, he seldom had, or seemed to want, more than one really close friend at a time. He impressed male acquaintances as being sophisticated but totally unassuming. When he moved on, as he frequently did, friendships languished because Anderson seldom wrote or answered letters. While a few women found him too cocky, most found him attractive. They liked his face, with its wide mouth, short nose, and high cheekbones, which hinted at the Indian blood on his mother's side of the family. All this under a head of dark, wavy hair that he wore a little longer than was then the fashion. His weight hovered at 140 pounds, trim and muscular. He kept in shape with long walks and tennis. He dressed carefully and well. Wherever fate took him all his life, Anderson would meet women who found him irresistible.

He read a great deal, mostly magazines up to 1930. He liked a good joke, and most of those he heard around the newsroom were bawdy; he hardly ever laughed aloud, usually just grinning, occasionally snickering. Newsrooms were noisy places, but away from them he was easily startled and hated noise. He liked hillbilly music. Food meant little to him; he ate only to live and tended to snack on crackers, onions, and tomato juice, which he kept in a desk drawer. His feet would sweat the day before he came down with a bad cold. In the privacy of his own lodgings, he liked to hang up his clothes and lounge around naked.

Traits, quirks, habits—add these and a hundred more together to get human character, personality. And somehow, Anderson's character seemed able to succeed only in the hard times of the 1930s.

His background was surely perfect for a writer destined to chronicle the desperate times of the working class. After Anderson's birth on June 19, 1905, in Weatherford, Texas, his family began a series of wanderings and short stays in many small towns in Texas and Oklahoma. His father was a printer, and the future novelist's earliest memories were of his father taking him to a print shop, where he would fall asleep on a stack of newsprint while his dad worked. He still managed to learn something about printing.

Finally the Andersons lit for a time in Ardmore, Oklahoma, where Eddie (as his family called him) grew up. Those were happy days. He took boxing lessons, and his ring debut was his lone professional match, which, of his family, only his father had the nerve to attend. Although he fought his opponent to a draw, Eddie never bothered to follow up. Teenage interests shoot in all directions, but they seldom shoot far.

"When I was sixteen," Anderson liked to recall, "I ran off with the mayor's son and my best friend to the harvest fields of Kansas. We rode freight trains." Anderson returned to work on the *Ardmorite,* but when summer came around again he chucked reporting to join a carnival band as tailgate trombonist. Finally he settled down to newspapering for the rest of the twenties, gypsying through ten towns in Oklahoma, Arkansas, and Texas before hitting Houston. There, he boasted to friends that, although he was only twenty-five, he had al-

E. H. Anderson, Edward's father   Edward as a teenager
                                         in Ardmore, Oklahoma

ready worked on twenty-six rags. Kissing a newspaper job good-bye
was an old habit.

Eddie had just missed the boat for the Lost Generation. Malcolm
Cowley, chronicler of America's literary scene in the twentieth century, says the members of that happily doomed crew graduated, or
might have graduated, from college between 1915 and 1922, when Eddie was just finishing high school. However, now that Melba had
turned him down, he was hell-bent on making the compulsory Lost
Generation pilgrimage to Europe.

After giving notice to the *Houston Post,* Anderson would have little
difficulty finding a berth on a Europe-bound freighter. Of the annual
$300 million in cargo that left Texas ports, most of it sailed from Hous-
ton and nearby Galveston. In spite of the 1900 storm and flood that
had almost wiped the city off its sandy barrier island, Galveston was
still the chief port of Texas. By 1930, however, an increasing number
of Atlantic ships were bypassing Galveston and chugging fifty miles
more to the Port of Houston via the thirty-foot-deep ship channel that
five years before had been created by widening and deepening the San
Jacinto River and Buffalo Bayou.

Anderson's departure on his freighter went unnoticed, unlike the departure of, say, Dorothy Parker (whose poetry Anderson mentioned derisively in his first novel), who also sailed for Europe in 1930. An established writer and Algonquin Circle wit, Parker embarked slightly tipsy on an ocean liner after reading proof on her book of short stories, *Laments for the Living.* Both Anderson and Parker were late, very late. Boatloads of American writers, composers, and painters had sailed to the Old World in the dozen years following the Great War, but now the expatriates' allowances from home were drying up because of the Wall Street Crash of 1929, and most were, or would soon be, trying to wrangle their passages back to the States.

The trip was certainly no luxury cruise for Anderson. He soon fell into the sailor's pattern of measuring out his life by watches, those four-hour intervals marked by the striking of the ship's bell. He learned that such humdrum activities as bathing and reading aboardship must be approached with renewed care, always subject to the moods of the North Atlantic. The work was hard and healthy. He had the opportunity to rethink his life in the silences of the morning watch between four and eight o'clock, black silences broken only by the dim starlight and the creaking of the ship straining across the ocean depths.

Anderson's ship docked in Belgium, in his and the world's eyes still the violated and heroic Belgium of 1914. He did not cross the North Sea to Scandinavia, although Norwegian and Swedish writers would one day change his philosophy and his life. Instead he visited France, where the "Poincaré prosperity" would continue through the year, where the strongest army in Europe kept an eye on the Germans. And Anderson looked at Germany, batted down by defeat, economy disintegrating, industrial production halved during the twelve months following the Wall Street Crash. Chancellor Heinrich Brüning would have to call an election in July, but Anderson, like most Americans, could know little of the growing political strength of an army veteran named Adolf Hitler, who lived in a luxurious nine-room apartment on the Prinzregentenstrasse in Munich.

Anderson neither knew nor cared. In a plain, working-class restaurant, a glass of red wine at hand, an apple sprinkled with cheese for dessert, Anderson would take more interest in the sight of a pretty girl walking along the other side of the cobblestone street.

2. Pulp Prose

━━

When Anderson's ship again docked at a Texas port, he went home. Home meant a little red-brick bungalow at 258 Graham Street in Abilene, a small city that had sprung up on the rolling prairielands of West Texas a half century earlier. His return delighted his parents. And if there was a touch of the return of the prodigal in the occasion, his stay-at-home sisters raised no jealous questions; they had always idolized Edward and tried to spoil him.

His father had a solid job, earning enough to buy groceries and make payments, so Black Thursday on Wall Street had seemed as remote as a flood in China. Money had of course tightened up in Abilene in the months following October 29, 1929, but things did not immediately seem worse. Money had been tight, much tighter than the local chamber of commerce liked to admit, for some time before the crash. The reason was simple: 75 percent of Abilene's economy in 1930 was based on agriculture, and farmers had never pulled out of the slump that hit them after World War I. The twenties did not roar much in West Texas farm towns. Elzie Robbins, who graduated from an Abilene business college in November of 1927, observed that many of his classmates took jobs "just for room and board." Young Robbins jumped at a modest position offered him by Farmers and Merchants Bank: "You couldn't even get a dishwasher's job in 1927." Eventually the Great Depression added more economic pain to Abilene, and city officials responded by urging everyone with a job to employ less fortunate citizens for odd jobs. Another young bank employee, W. O. Norman, recalled hiring men for yard work that he would have felt more comfortable doing himself. Wages would be cut and staffs trimmed, but few Abilene businesses would fail. Many homes would be repossessed, the Abilene State Bank would go under, and Central State Bank would be absorbed by Farmers and Merchants Bank. If Edward wanted to write in Abilene, he would not be distracted by tempting job offers.

The elder Andersons and their four children sat down to supper that first evening with a hundred topics to explore, a thousand questions to ask. Edward told them that he wanted to write for magazines. Where could Eddie set up to write and where would he sleep? Things were different now in the house, because all three of the Anderson girls were out of school and working; they needed as much private space as the little two-bedroom red-brick house could give. His mother thought that he might like to move into their one-room garage apartment, also of red brick but separate from the house, a place where he could have a little privacy and could peck at his typewriter at three o'clock in the morning without disturbing anyone. Edward's mother, Ellen Sexton Anderson, ran the house, and people said she ran the family too. Everybody agreed that the garage was ideal.

Papa wanted to know if Edward had seen any print shops in Europe and if they used handspiked type or these newfangled Linotypes. E. H. Anderson had not learned the printer's craft until he was getting on toward thirty, and then, after he learned, they sprang the Linotype on him. The son of a Weatherford architect, Edward Houston Anderson had refused a chance to go to college, had served with the 39th U.S. Volunteer Infantry in the Spanish American War, and had returned home to become what his family called a "playboy," although the word conjures a picture rather more fashionable than life in Weatherford, Texas, at the turn of the century might justify. Then he fell in love with Ellen Sexton, pretty and much younger, half Indian. She often made decisions on impulse and then put all her strong will behind them; her son would inherit some of that. They married in 1904, when E. H. was twenty-seven, when Ellen was fifteen.

Edward's father was an easygoing man with a gentle wit, who looked forward to a bottle of his own home brew after shop hours. If he had a serious failing, it was his inelasticity of mind, and it was the reason for the family wanderings. He preferred a type case and compositor's stick to the end of his days, and when a Linotype machine moved into a shop, E. H. generally moved on. His son would also display an inability to change with the times.

Edward's three sisters, all unmarried and attractive, had questions too. How was the food in Europe? How did European professional women dress? Louise, just younger than Edward, and Dorothy, only sixteen, both worked in Abilene offices. Did he see any new dances over there? Jacques-Henri Lartigue, a photographer whose work has recorded the moods of the twentieth century, wrote that in the twenties, everybody was dancing, to "Embraceable You," to "On the Sunny Side of the Street." Edward's twenty-year-old sister conducted the Imogene Anderson School of Dance at 266½ Cypress.

The family got up from the table and went into the living room. It was Eddie's turn to ask questions. Had anybody seen his old pal Charley Miller? Frank Grimes? Finally they adjourned to go to bed. Edward, suddenly weary, would try vaguely to make plans before dropping off to sleep in the middle of a thought.

After he got himself set up in the red-brick garage, with a bed, a desk, and a typewriter, Edward walked to town to say hello to his pals at the newspaper office on Cypress, just in case. A fellow might need a job if his magazine career didn't work out. Anderson felt he was in familiar territory the minute he stepped inside the narrow, three-story building, climbing the stairs past the business office on the first floor, past the composing room on the second, to the editorial department on the third.

There was Eddie's old friend Prexy Anderson, his face breaking into a grin. Prexy was a lean, short man. Harold was his Christian name, but the nickname "Prexy" had stuck so fast that he even used it as a byline. They had met back in 1926 when Eddie Anderson first appeared as the entire reportorial staff of the *Ranger Times,* a shirttail daily in a nearby oil-boom town. Eddie had been covering Ranger High football games, as had Prexy, who had only recently become sports editor for the *Abilene Morning News.* Since it was the custom of the time for a sportswriter to hurl at least one daily insult at his counterpart in a neighboring town, Eddie and Prexy exchanged conventional and meaningless unpleasantries even while becoming good friends.

"Editorial department" was a pretentious term for the cozy newsroom. The managing editor, Max Bentley, sat at his desk, his blue eyes focused on the sheet in his typewriter. He looked up over his glasses to see Eddie, and his expression softened. He stood up, a slender man in a dark gray suit, 5'11", graying brown hair. It's great to see you, Eddie. But I hope you aren't looking for a job. Times are so tough that they're talking about letting go some of the people we already have.

The classic newsroom social maneuver with a visiting journalist was to suggest a cup of coffee. The staff members involved — in this case Max Bentley and Prexy — got an extra cup in good conscience that way. A few steps across Cypress was the Grace Hotel Coffee Shop, where they could settle back and talk, and at its door they would say good-bye, which would keep the visitor from lingering in the newsroom, disrupting work.

So whatever happened to old man Scott? (M. T. Scott, the composing-room superintendent, had not liked Eddie much since his son and Eddie double-dated with two Abilene girls to a dance forty miles north in Stamford — and Eddie abandoned his date there. Telephoned by a worried mother in the middle of the night, M. T. had yanked his guilty son into the family car and driven back to Stamford to fetch the girl.) Scott was still in the shop. Maureen Eastus? (A McMurry College student hired to write "women's news," she had sparkling blue-gray eyes and fixed her hair like movie star Nancy Carroll's. Eddie had tried his line on Maureen, even taken her home once or twice, but all it got him was the jealous dislike of two rivals on the staff.) Got her degree, but still with us.

Other old times came up, Max remembering when Eddie covered the 1928 trial of the Santa Claus bank robber in Cisco; Prexy remembering when Eddie wrote "Lone Eagle Flying toward Sunrise" as a headline one May morning in 1927; Eddie remembering when he helped Max cover Lindbergh's visit to Abilene in September of 1927.

Publisher Bernard Hanks had hired Max Bentley in 1926 to establish a morning paper in Abilene to match his evening *Daily Reporter.* Originally from Abilene, Bentley had attracted national attention as managing editor of the *Houston Chronicle* when it waged a campaign against the Ku Klux Klan. He had then joined *McClure's* magazine in 1923 and commuted between Abilene and New York for three years. Hanks lured him to establish the *Abilene Morning News* with a salary more than twice that paid any of his other editors.

Before Eddie left the *Morning News* in 1929, he had gotten to know Bentley well. Now, sitting here a year later over coffee, Anderson would feel encouraged by Max's success. Bentley had published in the great American magazines. If Max could, Eddie could.

Back in the red-brick garage Edward Anderson rolled himself a cigarette, lit it, sat down at his desk, and cranked paper into his type-writer. In the same way that every baseball fan feels capable of man-aging a major league team if given the chance, in the way every U.S. senator feels able to grasp the presidency if first given the right com-mittee chairmanship, so every journalist feels he or she could write saleable fiction if just given the time. Now Edward had the time. He had lots of good stories in his head, too. However, after a few days he discovered that writing fiction in nothing like writing an obituary, an account of a football game, or the description of a two-headed calf.

Edward heard about another young Abilene writer who had sold stories to the pulpwood magazines. After giving it some thought, Ed-ward finally put down the book he had been reading, ambled out of the garage and across the backyard to the rear entrance of the An-derson house, through the kitchen and dining room to the hallway where a recessed nook held the family telephone. Consulting the tele-phone directory, he dialed 3482. (The "number please" of the local operator had vanished in the twenties.) A deep voice at the other end identified itself as John H. Knox.

I'm interested in writing fiction, and I hear you've sold some.

Well, some pulps, I've sold some pulps.

In the thirties, *Weird Tales, Thrilling Western, Black Mask,* and the like elbowed their betters on every drugstore rack. Although the pulp magazine traced its ancestry to the dime novels that began after the Civil War, its form in the thirties was established at the turn of the century, when Frank Munsey printed his new adventure magazine, the *Argosy,* on cheap pulp paper that yellowed almost before you could read through an issue. The old *Saturday Evening Post* was not noted for its deep intellectual fiction, but most of the pulps made *Post* stories sound like Henry James. Yet many able American writers got started there: Raymond Chandler, Dashiell Hammett, Ray Bradbury, Ten-nessee Williams, Paul Gallico, Philip Wylie, and MacKinlay Kantor, to name a few. Before his death a half century later, John H. Knox would estimate that, of the two million words he himself had pub-lished, more than half were in the pulps.

Rather than hopping a streetcar or borrowing the family auto, An-derson would choose to set out northeast on foot, along the sidewalk, toward the Knox place a little more than a half mile away. He was headed for the First Presbyterian Church, where John's father, the

Reverend Dr. T. S. Knox, had been pastor since 1912. Anderson walked briskly, but without too much hurry. Time stretched out all around him like a great inland lake; time had not yet become a river charging toward the sea.

Not much of a churchgoer himself, Anderson did not mind that John was the son of a Calvinist preacher. Abilene was a town with more than its share of preachers, most of them fundamentalist. Three things that newcomers always noticed about Abilene were fundamentalism, the optimism of its people, and the harshness of the land where they had settled.

At about the time Abilene was established in the 1880s, the fundamentalist movement was born in tent and brush arbor revivals. The revivalists were not strong on theological abstractions, but fundamentalists got together in 1900 to agree on five basic tenets, each of them a bullet aimed at modernism and Darwinism. Few Christians disagreed with the first four — tenets such as the divinity of Christ — but the fifth was the divider: affirmation of the literal truth of every word of the Bible. The hellfire sermons that hailed down from most Abilene pulpits added to these five a strong dose of Victorian morality. In Abilene, fundamentalism also meant teetotalism. Codicils condemned card playing, social dancing, Sunday movies, jazz saxophonists, paintings of naked women, and other traditional sins. Fundamentalism spread through many Protestant churches nationwide, but it was particularly virulent among Methodists and Baptists. In Abilene the Baptists, Methodists, and a third, smaller, Calvinist-toned group, the Churches of Christ, had set up colleges that offered education suffused with fundamentalism.

The optimism had carried over the from city's birth on March 15, 1881, as a real-estate promotion. The *Abilene Reporter,* sheltered in a tent, began boosting the town by cranking out editorials, just three months after Jay Gould's Texas & Pacific Railroad auctioned off the first batch of town lots. In 1906 Abilene promoters organized the Twenty-five Thousand Club, dedicated to achieving that figure in population, though by 1930 the city was still two thousand below that mark. When cotton plummeted to three cents a pound that year, the year Edward Anderson returned from Europe, even optimists paused. Yet pessimism was a luxury only easterners could afford. The late historian Arnold J. Toynbee, who believed that great civilizations are created when the people rise to adversity, would have liked the way Abilene citizens planted human culture on the scant topsoil of their nearly treeless land.

It took both stern religion and extreme optimism to shape Abilene on the low western plains, where occasional gullywashers relieved rainless spells. Although yearly rainfall averaged 23.59 inches, farmers and ranchers had to tough out years of below-normal rainfall, such as 1917, when only 10.85 inches fell. After the Civil War, the U.S. Cavalry had managed to gentle the Comanches and herd them off to Oklahoma, but they could not gentle the land itself. When a 1930s Abilene family drove out into the countryside for a picnic, mama could expect little shade from the runty mesquite trees, and papa would warn the kids about stepping on rattlesnakes. A quilt to keep the sand out of the potato salad would be spread on the beachlike riverbed; West Texas rivers are wet only after heavy rainstorms.

John H. Knox, like Edward, lived in a small, detached room behind the parsonage at 426 Orange. He answered Edward's knock, and John turned out to be a six-foot bear of a man, with a broad face and broad brow.

Edward entered a study that obviously served also as a bedroom. A table supported a well-broken-in typewriter on which Anderson would later see Knox punch out stories rapidly, using only two fingers. There were many books, their spines imprinted with such alien names as Fyodor Dostoyevsky, Marcel Proust, Louis-Ferdinand Celine, Thomas Mann, Knut Hamsun, Ivan Turgenev, Gustave Flaubert, mixed with the less exotic F. Scott Fitzgerald and Ernest Hemingway. Anderson had heard of some of them, read only a few.

Knox loaded his pipe. Anderson rolled a cigarette. The talk began, tentative and cautious at first. Soon Anderson relaxed enough to lay out his problems with fiction. John, watching him closely, decided Edward was serious about writing. They discovered they were both born in 1905. Their positions within their families were also roughly similar. Like Edward, John was the oldest child and the only son; Edward had three younger sisters, John had four.

Being a preacher's son had its problems but also its advantages. When John was a child, his father had read Shakespeare to him and had encouraged him to write when he grew older. After finishing high school at sixteen, John had signed up for three courses at Abilene Christian College. He couldn't finish them. He chucked formal edu-

John H. Knox, about 1935

cation for two years to thumb rides and hop freights across the continent, working in railroad shops, oil fields, lumber camps, and even as an assistant cameraman on silent films in Hollywood. Back from his wanderings, John tried Abilene Christian for another four academic quarters.

In the fall of 1924 John transferred to McMurry College across town. The change agreed with him. He flung himself into student publications. A paragraph from the yearbook says: "The last bell rang fifteen minutes ago. John will be coming pretty soon. He has probably been dreaming about his poem that appeared in Brief Stories Magazine, or perhaps he has been 'shieking' across to Pat's Place." That single, good, final year was all the academe he wanted. He turned down a newspaper job and went to work as a shoe clerk while he began his assault on the pulp fiction market.

In this new friend Anderson found someone with whom to discuss the problems confronting every fiction writer. Perhaps even more important, Knox would introduce Anderson to contemporary books worthy of serious attention.

3. Young Minds of Abilene

When his back grew weary after hours at his typewriter, Edward Anderson got up and walked out, east, toward the library. In 1930 the Carnegie Library was Abilene's Mermaid Tavern, Kit-Cat Club, Bloomsbury salon, and Algonquin Dining Room. The town's young writers hung out there because the Carnegie librarian welcomed anyone with a claim, no matter how vague, to being a writer and because it was cheaper than a table in a mom-and-pop cafe, where a fellow had to part with a nickel for a cup of coffee. After a refreshing seven-minute walk Edward reached the old-fashioned building: lawn and trees outside, yellow-brick walls, tile roof, two stories stacked on a basement in which back issues of magazines were stored. Edward passed between two Doric columns to enter the glass double doors.

He smiled at the pretty assistant — her name was Emily — who was helping a woman check out a volume. The most read books of 1930 were *Cimarron* by Edna Ferber, *Exile* by Warwick Deeping, and *The Woman of Andros* by Thornton Wilder. Few had heard of *Flowering Judas* by Katherine Anne Porter, born in nearby Brown County; in New York Porter stewed because Harcourt, Brace had published a measly six hundred copies of it. Carnegie patrons were more likely to be asking for a book by a University of Texas professor named J. Frank Dobie; his *Coronado's Children* was a Literary Guild selection that year.

Lights, converted from gas to electricity, hung above the tables in the library's two wings. Signs on the bookshelves guided the browser; John Knox's favorite sign was "Philosophy and Parlor Games." A few of the Carnegie's twelve thousand volumes, such as those by Dreiser and Hemingway, were considered a threat to public morals and kept locked up, or "in jail" as the young writers used to call it.

When Anderson caught sight of Knox sitting at their customary table in the southeast corner of the reading room, he ambled over. It was there that John introduced Edward to many of Abilene's literary hopefuls. Writing was just a temporary enthusiasm with some of them, the poet Oswald Babb, for example, whose father would soon put him to work in the wholesale grocery business. Babb eventually became an investment banker, writing to Knox from his home in France. A more serious writer was Files Bledsoe, whom Knox called "a studied bohemian, but sound, not an empty poseur." Only twenty-three at the time, Bledsoe was always making plans to write a biography of Lafcadio Hearn, always making conversation about it instead. Later he would work as a publicist for dancer Ruth St. Denis in England, collaborating with her on *An Unfinished Life*. He would also write for the *Daily Worker* in New York and be investigated by the FBI; help edit the magazine of the Partido Revolucionario Institucional in Mexico, where he would also publish a successful novel, *Lluvia y Fuego*; and publish many translations from the Spanish.

Through Knox, Anderson got to know Houston Heitchew, the great-grandson of General Sam Houston, the victor of San Jacinto and the first president of the Republic of Texas. Heitchew never mentioned his great forebear, in fact flared up in anger if anybody mentioned him. A gangling youth so thin he looked even taller than his six feet, Heitchew had the sallow complexion of those whose faces are seldom turned from their books. When Heitchew had finished high school, a group of Abilene men had offered to pay for his studies at Yale or Harvard, but he would have none of it.

Heitchew was the shrewdest analyst and critic of the Carnegie group. "Houston was like this," explained Knox. "He would work harder for something that didn't make money than for something that was profitable. If you happened to wonder aloud what part of the Great Pyramid of Egypt the bricks of the Wooten Hotel would make, Houston would show up in a week with it exactly figured." On occasion Heitchew applied his knife to an overgrown Knox short story, trimming without sapping it. Once historian W. Curry Holden, then teaching at McMurry, asked Knox to vet some chapters of Holden's first book, *Alkali Trails*. Knox passed it to Heitchew. "Believe me, they got a laundry job," Knox said. "There were no rings on the collar when Houston got through with them." Heitchew was just the critic to make intelligent suggestions on Anderson's early tries at fiction and just the type to end spectacularly. On September 2, 1943, Heitchew plunged mysteriously—many believed he jumped—from an open window on the fourteenth floor of the Wooten Hotel. He fell to his death on the Paramount Theater roof.

Edward was not long at the table with John and others before the librarian came over to say something pleasant. Her name was Maude E. Cole, and she was fifty-one the year Anderson got back from Europe. She was a plain-faced woman, kind looking, with a smile over a firm jawline. She wore rimless glasses, and her dark hair was cut short, parted, styled carefully but practically.

A widow since 1921, Mrs. Cole had first operated a hat shop and then a hotel flower shop before finding her real calling at the Carnegie. Being a librarian harmonized with her sense of order, and more important, it stimulated her creative juices. She had begun writing verse, which then appeared in the *New York Times,* the *Chicago Tribune,* and other newspapers and magazines. She believed it was her duty to fan every spark of literary activity in town.

The thirties, of course, was the era of the shushing librarian. Libraries banned the spoken sentence in favor of the printed paragraph, in favor of deep meditation, or even an occasional snore, so long as it was soft. Because of its jangle, a telephone had not been installed in the library. Yet while she kept most of the Carnegie's patrons to a whisper, Mrs. Cole let the city's writers talk at their own special table.

Some afternoons Mrs. Cole brought down her six-year-old grandson, A.C. Greene, a future author himself, who may have become a writer because he was impressed with the way his grandmother treated those writers at their special table. "My grandmother was very protective of the young writers who hung around at the library," Greene recalled. "The writers would get fairly loud, and I'm sure they would use four-letter words. She told me they were older, that they were grown up and could use that kind of language, but for me not to use it."

When other Carnegie patrons complained about talk at the writers' table, Mrs. Cole put the complainants firmly in their places: "They know what they're doing at that table. They're really using the library." Eventually, however, some of the complaints reached the library board.

The Carnegie board was Maude Cole's bogey. The library had been the creation, more or less, of the City Federation of Women's Clubs, which engineered a 1908 grant of nine thousand dollars from

Andrew Carnegie. The board consisted of clubwomen, and membership carried high-society overtones. These formidable matrons respected Mrs. Cole for her learning and ability, but they also regarded her as their creature, like the library janitor, or the washerwomen who starched their husbands' shirts. For Mrs. Cole, the board's day of solemn deliberations each month was a period of terror. She got up those mornings sick with apprehension, her fingers clumsy as she dressed herself, her temper short with her grandson. Some member of the board who had gone to the library to return, say, *Claire Ambler* by Booth Tarkington, and to check out *The Bishop Murder Case* by S. S. Van Dine, would have seen with her own eyes and, worse, heard with her own ears, the rowdy writers.

It was an era that dealt quickly and simply with certain types of vagrants who frequented the library, types with whom librarians in the last years of the twentieth century would find it more difficult to deal. In the thirties, among the newspapers and magazines no vagrant could doze; in the women's lounge no bag lady could nibble at a sandwich hoarded in her purse; behind the bookshelves no frustrated Romeo could lurk to peek between volumes at the legs of middle-aged women. The police in those days simply arrested such trespassers on library tranquillity. Talkative writers, however, some of whom were from Abilene's most respected families, were a different matter.

At the climactic board meeting, the chairwoman would save this hot item for last on the agenda, under "other business," in order to get through routine matters smoothly, before any unpleasantness. Nevertheless, she finally came to it. Someone, she would begin hesitantly, had mentioned that certain young persons who gathered in the Carnegie now and then were, well, perhaps without realizing it, talking loudly, sometimes rudely, and thereby disturbing scholars poring over texts. Of course, it should be understood that the library staff should in no way discourage young persons from coming in and reading to improve their minds, but. . . .

Not this time. At every whim of these hoity-toity guardians of Abilene's culture, Mrs. Cole had knuckled under. But not this time. These young persons are what the library is for, Maude Cole told them. They are using their minds. They are serious people who read books seriously. Only in the library do they have a place where they can openly discuss the intellectual questions of the day. Mrs. Cole felt deeply about it, and she spoke with obvious emotion.

The board backed down. The issue never came up again.

Knox and his cronies asked Mrs. Cole to get some of the more intellectual magazines and newspapers. She managed to find money in her meager budget to subscribe to two or three "just for you boys." One was the *Red Express,* published in San Antonio and filled with radical-left editorials and exposés on such subjects as the cigar makers' strike.

A small auditorium occupied the top floor of the Carnegie. One day Maude's grandson followed two of the writers up the stairs to the empty auditorium. Little A.C. took a front-row center seat to watch the pair, scripts in hand, act out a scene one of them had written. Theater magic! A half century later A.C. Greene would muse over the performance, the names of player and author just beyond the edge of his memory.

This was a time of experiment for Anderson, who even tried his hand at poetry. He mentioned his poems to Knox, but he never showed them to anybody. Anderson had returned to Abilene too late to take part in *Harlequinade,* one of those ephemeral fixtures of twentieth-century letters known as "little magazines." It began in 1929 and expired with its twelfth issue, in 1930. In appearance *Harlequinade* was modest, its contents punched out on a typewriter and badly mimeographed. Volume one, with all twelve issues, totaled only 136 pages, mostly poetry, drawings, and essays. Maude Cole was an associate editor and contributed several poems. *Harlequinade* fizzled about the time its young editor, Francis Finberg (who signed his poems "Franz A. Finberg") followed his father to Lubbock to trade in cotton. Francis was a recent Simmons graduate. Hair thinning even in youth, he wore one of those raccoon coats dear to the Jazz Age types depicted in George Held cartoons. Knox, who had himself edited a couple of little magazines, *Tom-Tom* and *Troubadour,* told Anderson that Finberg was a lightweight, "just a coonskin coat with a voice." Knox's name was not included among those of *Harlequinade* contributors.

What happened to all the good talk that once enlivened the Carnegie? Perhaps it was not so deep, nor so witty as the imagination renders it, but its mere existence at all is interesting. Writing of the conversation of another group of young writers, the Bloomsbury group, Virginia Woolf lamented that it was as elusive as smoke, that it flew up the chimney and vanished.

John Knox became a familiar visitor at the Anderson home. Handsome and pleasant, with natural good manners, John was welcomed by E. H., Ellen, and their daughters. John's favorite among the three pretty girls was Imogene, the dance teacher, tall and gracefully slender. "Imogene has a rare personality and a ready wit," said her Abilene High yearbook. "She sparkled and bubbled her way through high school." John's favorite was not smitten, however; she was already in love with a young medical student named Leon Hodges, whom she would later marry.

Waiting around for Eddie, John listened to several anecdotes from Imogene that showed another side of her brother. There was, for instance, the night Eddie came in late from the Ardmore newspaper and woke Imogene up. "It was raining outside, and Eddie pulled this little kitten out of his pocket that was just about drowned. Eddie said, 'I found him about to be washed down the sewer.'" Imogene had jumped up to help her brother dry the kitten and feed it.

Imogene said that in high school Eddie had been popular. "My friend Mary, she just adored Edward. She would want to come and spend the night with me, but not because of me, because of Edward." Edward had taken private lessons on the trombone and played in the high-school band. "He would practice in the bathroom. It was hot in there, and he would come out just wringing wet." He had learned of Imogene's own interest in dancing and, out of his own earnings, had paid for her early lessons with Ruth Miller in Ardmore.

Eddie had worked ever since Imogene could recall. "When he was tiny, they were building a hotel in Ardmore, and he got a job as waterboy." She also said Eddie had held "a man's job" as a reporter on the *Ardmorite* all the time he was in high school. "When he quit school the teachers would call and tell mama that he was brilliant, and that he needed to go to college." Edward quit, despite his family's protests, just a half credit short of his diploma. Imogene remembered well Edward's departure for Tulsa and the *World*. "He wore a navy blue suit, and a red tie, and a little derby hat, and he thought he was really something."

She told John that in 1927, when her father lost his job because the Ardmore weekly closed, Edward came to the rescue. "It was a shattering experience for my father. He was fifty. Edward was in Abilene, and he said, 'Daddy, y'all just come out here, and I'll get you an apartment, and I'll find you some kind of work!'"

Back in the red-brick garage, lounging in his chair against a wall, puffing his pipe, John talked with Eddie, who sat with spine bolt upright in his chair opposite and fingered a homemade cigarette. The two young men had often double-dated, and Eddie impressed girls as swaggering; he impressed their mothers as tough and dangerous. But to Knox he seemed open and friendly, yet with something held back, something not revealed.

Now and then they shared a pint of Prohibition booze, and when he was really drunk Eddie sometimes retold a curious incident from his early childhood. To punish him, his mother stood her son in a corner behind a chair. Eddie took a pencil and lettered an H on the back of the chair. It seemed beautiful to him, and he began embellishing the letter, giving it fancy strokes, serifs, and curls — but he finally made one stroke too many. He said he had kept on till he ruined it. Knox, who had read his Freud, would wonder if this hinted at darker things, hidden deep in the caverns of his friend's psyche.

Over on Hickory Street lived another young writer in the Carnegie group, Michael T. Looby, who later recalled: "It was mighty cold in Abilene that winter and there wasn't much we could do at night except sit around the fire and talk. Mostly we talked about literature after devoting a few minutes of each session to the settling of current world problems." Looby lived with his two sisters, both Simmons students, and his mother, the widow of a rancher. He had studied at Rice Institute in Houston and was employed by Zingery Map Company, although he would later drift into the newspaper business. He recalled that "after having sold stories to two (very) little magazines, one of which folded up immediately after printing my yarn, I was beginning to consider myself a budding Hemingway." The real commercial magazines, those that paid in money instead of copies (*Harlequinade* had boasted that it paid only in undying fame), proved as cool to Looby's efforts as to those of Anderson.

Knox had the edge on them. Knox had a real flair for writing the formulas of pulp fiction, perhaps not an altogether fortunate gift in the light of his more serious, long-term intentions, but Looby and Anderson would envy him nevertheless. Knox continued to sell, acquired an agent, and built a reputation among the editors of pulpdom. Anderson and Looby continued to get their manuscripts back, a little more dog-eared with each round-trip.

Then one day Anderson got a letter from a pulp editor accepting his prizefight story called "The Little Spic." Phoning his pals with the happy news wasn't his style. His way was to mosey down to see them after lunch, and in his everyday tone of voice, quiet and even, put the match to the skyrocket.

Success called for a party, which, among young intellectuals in 1931, translated into securing some bootleg bourbon. Knox's den was too close to the sermons of his father, and Looby lived with three females. Only Eddie's red-brick garage would be far enough from the puritan morality they despised.

They turned up the jazz a little louder on the radio. "And did we celebrate!" said Looby.

4. Hopping a Freight

An automobile whose license plates identified it as being from Abilene chugged into a small West Texas town one warm day in the second half of 1931. John H. Knox drove, and beside him in the passenger seat rode Edward E. Anderson. The road ran right through the middle of the little town, a route which brought down the speed of motorists more effectively than all the signs that the Texas Highway Department might post. Knox guided the automobile with care, on the lookout for those ancient citizens whose driving habits and judgment, formed at horsetrot in the nineteenth century, misled them into nosing their cars out haphazardly from side streets into a stream of traffic that now rushed along at thirty miles an hour.

Within the city limits the paved highway turned into a brick street. They were early, so Knox and Anderson stopped at the first little roadside cafe they found. The greasy-spoon cafes of the thirties were primitive compared with a McDonald's or Dairy Queen, but they shared a kind of uniformity. Three tables covered by red-checked oilcloth. A long, low counter with, on the owner's side of it, a glass case containing slices of pie ranging from apple to egg custard to pecan and back again. Men on stools at the counter. Two cups of java. A grandmotherly waitress, with white hair and in a shapeless print dress, running the place by herself while her husband ran errands or maybe, unknown to her, sneaked a hand or two of moon at the local domino parlor. Knox and Anderson had flirted with their share of waitresses, but they wouldn't give someone they considered to be a tough old hen a second look.

The friends had plenty to talk about:

The weather. How long would it be before a man could no longer sleep comfortably outside?

Letters. The arrangements for swapping talk by mail would be hard to figure out. Anderson almost never wrote anyone anyway.

Small talk. J. B. Priestley had recently published *Angel Pavement*, a British novel of the working class akin to some of the American proletarian novels beginning to come off the press.

When customers finished their coffee, waitresses didn't offer a refill. They were tighter with coffee, those tough waitresses who lived in the back rooms of their own eating joints. Still talking, Knox and Anderson got up and walked out the door. No tip. Texans in the thirties would no more think of offering a tip to a waitress than they would think of trying to bribe a Texas Ranger.

Back in the car and driving toward the center of town again, they passed a junkyard, a big unpainted building with a tin roof and a sign that read Garage above its open double doors, a blacksmith shop, an open-front fruit-and-vegetable stand. Once downtown Knox turned onto one of the principal streets, past blocks of stores, past some shabby residences. They sighted the railway depot a block away, an impressive red structure.

Maybe we ought to drive on past and down the line a little.

So Knox turned and drove parallel to, but a block away from, the railway line for three blocks. He stopped and switched off the ignition.

Well, here it is.

The two men got out, Anderson reaching into the back to fish out a rough traveling bag filled with necessities. The two friends walked toward the railroad. Knox knew someone in Abilene who knew about train schedules. Sure enough, there was the freight, its engine fired, temporarily idling, with its string of cars snaking from the depot back along the rails, ready to continue its run. The two friends walked over to some nearby shade, Knox sitting down, and Anderson, a little tense, putting down his bag. The train began to move. Time for Knox to stand up and shake Anderson's hand. Anderson started to walk with that quick athletic step of his toward the slowly moving train. Several cars passed. Anderson broke into a trot to stay even with an empty freight car, tossed in his bag, braced his hands flat just inside the open door and vaulted up with a twist that landed him sitting. A final wave. Knox watched the train out of sight before turning and walking thoughtfully back to his car.

This parting began to take shape earlier in 1931. Eddie and John had been sitting at their desks, and pecking away for hours every day. (A veteran labor journalist of the era, Mary Heaton Vorst, said that the art of writing is the art of applying the seat of your trousers to a chair in front of a typewriter.) Between times they got together to talk. Maude Cole at the Carnegie had now and then done the unthinkable: invited them into the staff break room to drink a cup of librarian's coffee. Like the holy of holies in Solomon's temple, the break room was a simple place, devoid of most earthly treasures. An old breakfast table, some chairs, that was about it. Mrs. Cole and her young assistants ate their sack lunches there. She might even join John and Eddie — Emily, watch the desk for a few minutes, please — but John and Eddie would soon have to go outside for a smoke.

During these sessions they had gradually come to face the facts. The truth was that one short-story sale did not amount to a financially successful career in pulp magazines. All the other pulp submissions by Anderson continued to bounce. The truth was that Anderson couldn't quite get the hang of those adventure formulas. His feeling was for reality, which seldom speeds through the formulaic twists that lead to climax and resolution in popular fiction. In realistic writing you may isolate a sequence of events in time, isolate a sequence with a theme that appears, swells, and plays out, in a time frame as long as life or as short as a love affair. But that wasn't the stuff *Sport Story* or *G-8 and His Battle Aces* were made of. The truth was that Anderson could not write for pulps.

On the upside, Knox saw that his friend's style was the pure American language described by H. L. Mencken. Anderson wrote with a meat-and-potatoes wordstock, with the lean and simple syntax of such contemporaries as Dos Passos, Hemingway, and Chandler. It was a style stripped of the mandarinisms of the New Englanders, a style created almost simultaneously with the modern newspaper and somewhat mistakenly identified with it. When he knew a story (and this often meant he had to have seen it with his own eyes), Anderson could relate it with wonderful effect.

Knox also knew that his friend had an imagination that "could fantasize a hawk into a handsaw," but it was an imagination that dealt only with real humans, getting inside their souls to see how they would act — a musician forced to go hoboing, or an honorable farmhand who slides into banditry. Anderson's imagination was not cut out to deal with English noblemen who became tree-swinging apes or cowboys who spent more time gunfighting than herding cattle. As much as Anderson thought he wanted to write "popular junk," Knox realized that his friend would have to write serious fiction instead.

Like the character in Anderson's first novel who says of the protagonist, "I was shipmates with this guy. He reads all the time," Knox found his friend read "all the time." Trouble was, the public schools in Ardmore had not given Anderson's reading much direction into contemporary writing. American literature in Ardmore meant Nathaniel Hawthorne and the poetry of Henry Wadsworth Longfellow —obsolete language tangled with moral questions that failed to stir the writers of the Roaring Twenties. Like Ardmore, Anderson's textbooks were timid about focusing attention on the new, about bringing the list of significant writers up to date. When Knox got acquainted with him, Anderson had read Jack London, Jim Tully, and a lot of magazines and potboiling best-sellers. Anderson had thus been fortunate to fall in with the little group of Abilene writers and intellectuals. Knox had "encouraged him to read Knut Hamsun and the Russians." Maude Cole had been able to supply Anderson with the Carnegie copies of Constance Garnett's groundbreaking translations of Russian literature, which were introducing the English-speaking world to Goncharov, Tolstoy, Turgenev, Ostrovsky, Dostoyevsky, and Chekhov. Those same translations had influenced writers as diverse as Arnold Bennett (who died the year Anderson hopped that fateful freight) and Hemingway (who himself was to publish a proletarian novel of sorts— *To Have and Have Not*—in the late thirties). Russia's great writers looked at reality unflinchingly, without romanticizing— an attitude likely to appeal to an honest journalist. Knox would also introduce Anderson to *The Lower Depths,* as well as such radical works as *Das Kapital* and *The Intelligent Woman's Guide to Socialism.* The characters in Anderson's first book would talk about Maxim Gorki, George Bernard Shaw, and Karl Marx as well as Tully and London.

Anderson had found that he particularly liked the novels of Knut Hamsun. Knox thought that "the old Norwegian wizard, though his tricks were inimitable, was a good influence on Eddie, who had a knack of his own for conjuring immediacy." In the short run Hamsun's influence helped Anderson; over the long haul his influence may have been less than positive.

A curious figure in the world of letters, Hamsun was born in 1859 at Lom in Norway and from the age of four lived with an uncle on the remote Lofoten Islands. He apprenticed as a cobbler but published a long poem and a novel when he was nineteen. While trying to write during the following years, he worked at various lowly jobs in Norway and later in the United States, where legend says he was fired as a Chicago streetcar conductor because he was reading Euripides on the rear platform instead of letting passengers on and off. Then in 1888 Hamsun published a fragmentary novel, *Hunger*, in a Danish magazine, and it brought him fame in his twenty-ninth year. With this and other great works that followed—*Mysteries* (1892); *Pan* (1894), *Victoria* (1898), and *Growth of the Soil* (1917)—Hamsun explored the psychology, primarily the subconscious psychology, of his protagonists and was constantly preoccupied with the lyrical nuances of feeling.

When World War I erupted, Hamsun sided openly with the kaiser and Germany. Like George Bernard Shaw, William Butler Yeats, H. G. Wells, Ezra Pound, and many other writers, he scorned liberal democracy. Two years after the war, this shy, puzzling man won a Nobel Prize for literature. Hamsun's fame was at its zenith in the twenties and thirties.

With the outbreak of World War II, Hamsun again sided with the Germans, and he even went so far as to visit the Führer in 1943. When Germany invaded Norway, Hamsun exhorted his countrymen to "throw away your rifles and return home. The Germans are fighting for us and all neutrals." At war's end he and his wife escaped prosecution as collaborators only because of his age and mental condition. In his pre-war heyday *Living Age* had said that "no living writer has a soul that bruises more easily." After the war, thousands sent his books back to him. Hamsun died in 1952, rejected and scorned; only after forty years had passed would his reputation show signs of emerging from the cloud.

Anderson and Knox, in their bull sessions, had often talked of Hamsun and other writers, sometimes of women, sometimes of their own ambitions or pasts. Anderson showed particular interest in the year Knox spent as a bindle stiff, when he took French leave from college to wander over the West and Northwest. Knox had earned his keep in lumber camps, railroad shops, and oil fields in Washington, Oregon, and California and even served as a messman on a Swedish ship.

Knox had returned with plenty of good yarns, for example, his getting the job as an assistant cameraman with a Hollywood film company. Everybody "doubled in brass" on film crews back then, and one day when an actor failed to show up, the director asked Knox to play the part of a man drowning in the ocean off Catalina Island. As John told it, observers later congratulated him on playing the part so well that an old lady on the pier witnessed his drowning act and fainted from excitement and fright.

Anderson had a few road tales of his own to tell Knox, such as when he was a teenager and had hopped freights to follow the wheat harvest. Also there had been that summer tooting his trombone with the carnival band. He had rather liked his small tastes of life on the road. Perhaps because of these experiences, Anderson had become fascinated by the hordes of unemployed men who rode their "side-door Pullmans" through Abilene. Jobs vanished as the economic wheels almost ceased to turn in late 1931, and across the nation 305 banks went bust in September, 522 in October. As the year drew to an end, 10 million were unemployed. Reduced to being poor, many hopped freights. "When you're poor, and you stand in one place, trouble just seems to catch up with you," one hobo of the era states. Nobody knows how many were in motion along the rails. The Missouri Pacific officially noted 186,028 freight riders in 1931, and there were lots they didn't see. In a half year, 45,000 clung to rolling stock going through El Paso. Kansas City had 1,500 passing through its rail yards daily. One survivor of this hard life told Studs Terkel that the hoboes developed "a coyote mentality."

Anderson's interest in hoboing paralleled a growing American interest in gangsters. Edward G. Robinson would make film history in 1931 in the title role of *Little Caesar*. Edward Arnold also scored a Broadway success as gang leader Jake Dillon in *Whistling in the Dark*.

Although the newspapers noted that year that the Japanese had invaded Manchuria, Anderson would not pay much attention. Nor would the rest of the nation; America's mind was on its own troubles. Few inside Germany even could know that on September 17 Adolf Hitler had refused to let his blond niece (and early love) Geli Raubel return to her voice studies, and that on the following day she was found dead in her apartment.

History spun on, but the events that Edward Anderson noticed were the arrivals of the postman carrying new rejection slips. Eddie finally despaired. He had thus decided to go hoboing himself, to break away, to go adventuring, to gather material for a serious novel.

5. Hoboes

Two years later Anderson turned up in New York. He had spent those years in the twilight world of vagabonds, riding the side-door Pullmans across the nation—San Francisco, Chicago, New Orleans, Boston. Now and then he turned to riding his thumb along the highways, although he felt that hitchhiking was "like sticking your tail out and every time somebody passes they kick it." He got tired of the hobo life and decided to try to land a New York newspaper job.

In the early thirties, every out-of-work Texas newspaperman who bummed through the East, dozens of them, hit up the great Stanley Walker for a job, or so it must have seemed to Walker. The Texas native was then at the height of his early prestige as city editor of the *New York Herald Tribune.* He was thirty-five years old in 1933, only seven years older than Anderson, but to a guy who had been hoboing Walker seemed godlike in the power of his position.

Walker had come to New York in 1919 with twenty dollars in his pocket and about six bits' worth of reportorial experience. During his three years at the University of Texas (where J. Frank Dobie was one of his profs), Walker had worked a little on the *Austin American.* Next came a brief stay at the *Dallas Morning News,* followed by a job as secretary to the mayor of Dallas. With this scant seasoning, Walker talked his way into a reporter's job at the old *New York Herald.* After its merger with the *Tribune* he became night city editor in 1926 and then city editor in 1928—before his thirtieth birthday. Alexander Woollcott, then barely a notch below H. L. Mencken as an oracle of the age, called Walker "the most notable city editor of his time." *Literary Digest* said Walker was the most written-about city editor in the United States. Walker published his first book, *Night Club Era,* in 1933, and when Anderson went to see him, Walker was already at work on what is perhaps his best book, *City Editor,* which would be published the following year. Several critics have compared the Walker prose style in these books to that of Mencken.

The meetings with Walker stayed vividly in Anderson's mind and appeared later in the novel he wrote about the hobo wanderings of a protagonist called Acel Stecker, a musician. In the novel Acel lands in New York and asks Red Gholson for help in finding a job. Gholson, who is "really a big shot" in the music world, is said to be from Stecker's hometown; Walker was from Lampasas, Texas, but his wife was from Anderson's own Abilene. Her name was Tot Sandefer, and she taught briefly at Simmons University in Abilene, where her father was president, before going to New York to establish the maternity shop at Lord and Taylor.

When he went to the *Herald Tribune* to see his fellow Texan, Anderson worried, as the character Stecker did in his similar interview, about his scuffy shoes and general appearance. "I hope he doesn't smell gasoline or whatever it is they cleaned this suit of mine with. That's the trouble with four-bit cleaning."

The city editor got on well with the *Herald Tribune* staffers he directed, correcting their errors with wisecracks, earning their respect for his intelligence and intuition. Walker and Anderson also hit it off. Along with having similar backgrounds, Walker and Anderson were both relatively small and wiry, spoke with low, even voices, avidly followed boxing, and enjoyed walking for exercise. They had mutual friends such as Max Bentley to talk about. Anderson was surprised that Walker seemed proudest of his first fiction sale, which was to one of the old Munsey pulps that routinely published John Knox's stories.

Down to business, Anderson asked about a job. Like the big shot who interviews Stecker in the novel, Walker reminded Anderson that "times are pretty hard here in New York now. Lots of boys out of work now."

"Yes I know. I tell you, just any sort of job would put me on my feet."

"You are not particular then?"

"Oh, no. To tell you the truth, I hoboed it up here. Anything would look good to me."

"Lots of boys are out of work. Some very good boys are out of work now."

"I know things are tough, all right."

"I tell you what, then. Where are you staying?"

"I'm staying at the Seafarers' Home. It's a pretty reasonable place."

"Well, I'll see if I can't dig you up something. You give me a ring in a week or so."

Cheered, the job seeker walked away from the interview and down the busy street: "By god, by god, by god. . . ."

For more than two months, Anderson checked with Walker every Monday or Tuesday. Those were the early months of the Roosevelt administration in Washington, and while he was waiting, Anderson decided to make a quick hobo jaunt to the nation's capital to view the New Deal firsthand. He spent four days there and later wrote Melba Newton in Houston that "if there is another newspaperman who bummed the press gallery in the senate, I've never heard of him. But I did, and you may be sure I didn't look like a pulp fictioneer's rod-riding hero, either."

Walker was unable to find work for his fellow Texan, and when Anderson left New York in late 1933 the two men lost touch. In 1935, the year Walker's third book, the cynical *Mrs. Astor's Horse,* came out, he resigned his city editorship at the *Herald Tribune.* During the late thirties and forties, he held various high editorial posts with the *New York Daily Mirror,* the *New York American, New Yorker* magazine, and the *Philadelphia Evening Public Ledger* and even returned to the *Herald Tribune* for a time. He also wrote freelance pieces for the top magazines of the era, such as the frequently reprinted "Decline of the Newspaper Souse." In a notable article for *Look* magazine, he smashed and ripped Philadelphia. Always conservative in politics and an admirer of Republican Thomas E. Dewey, Walker caused a national stir in 1944 with his book, *Dewey, an American of This Century.*

Walker married another journalist, Ruth Alden Howell, and they left New York in the mid-fifties to settle in Texas, where he wrote such books as *Home to Texas* and *Texas.* In 1962 a medical specialist told Walker that he suffered from cancer of the throat and would have to have his larynx removed. One Sunday morning in November, about a month after his sixty-fourth birthday, Walker turned a shotgun on himself. He died in the same area in which he was born.

During this period of hoboing Anderson typically wrote few letters, and most of those he did write went to Melba Newton in Houston. He seldom communicated with his family back in Abilene, and not at all with his pal John Knox.

Knox and Anderson's primary pursuit had of course been literature, but a strong second was pretty girls. They shared names and telephone numbers. They double-dated. A young woman who knew them both talked about Anderson's "low-slung good looks" and his almost infuriatingly cocky self-assurance, while she termed Knox "gentlemanly" and "very handsome."

After Anderson had hopped the freight out of West Texas, a woman named Mabel Bishop Kimble moved from Dallas to Abilene. She, like the character Anderson called the Baroness in his first novel, set up as a private teacher of "expression," a term of the era meaning poetry recitation and public speaking. Mabel was a tall, slender woman with an olive complexion and large, dramatic, brown eyes. She wore her hair straight, drawn back and bound. Like many persons who make a strong impression on the stage or at the lectern, her face spoke in a theatrical way without her uttering a word. She was divorced, a condition that at that time carried with it a heavy aura of romantic wickedness. She was the mother of a child who had remained with her husband. She was older than John Knox. Finally, like the doomed heroines of so many nineteenth-century novels, plays, and operas, Mabel suffered from tuberculosis. This "Camille's consumption" was arrested, but she took medicine for it daily. While she coached her students in expressive public speech, in private Mabel said little, enigmatically keeping her own counsel. In sum, Mabel's personality consisted of a combination of things rich and strange enough to fascinate a young poet. John was hooked. He married her.

Aside from the usual difficulties of living with in-laws, it wouldn't have seemed right in the thirties for the son of a Calvinist minister to bring home a divorced woman as his bride. John and Mabel moved to Breckenridge, sixty miles northeast of Abilene.

About that time, halfway across the nation, Edward Anderson ran along beside a boxcar, reached out and took a firm hold on the lower rungs of its ladder, and pulled himself up. He did not want to end up like the fat guy with one leg, the one that the other bums had to hold up when he took a shower. Anderson crawled out on top of the freight car, hoping to find an open hatch. He was heading home, back to Abilene.

He had pages and pages of notes in his bag, notes on things like waiting in mission lines for a bowl of soup served after a sermon: "I just couldn't keep from thinking about it all the time he was preaching. Why in the hell didn't that prodigal son kill them hogs and eat?" Binging diners for donuts. Sleeping in parks: "I've been in Central Park and Boston Common and Grant Park and the Plaza in El Paso and Lafayette Square and Pershing Square." He had seen Battery Park in New York, where the sleeping bums "lay scattered on the grass like corpses on a battlefield."

In the course of things, Anderson talked with radical bindle stiffs who were skeptical about democracy. "The average man is just an alimentary canal with a billiard ball for a head." That year Machine-Gun Kelly kidnaped millionaire Charles F. Urschel in Oklahoma City. A bum comments: "They can kidnap them all if they want to. . . . They wouldn't spit on me if my guts were on fire." Some were out-and-out Reds: "Do you approve of a system that operates so one man can have enough to buy a billion meals and another can't raise the price of one?"

He saw grisly events, such as the fight between a big bum and a little bum in which a restaurant display window shattered, slashing the big guy: "The side of his face hung down on his shoulder." He met girls like those he eventually called "Corinne" and "Ann" in his first novel, girls who didn't waste a lot of time with hand-holding and other amorous elegances. "Ann says that a down-and-out man begs and a woman sells," Corinne remarks. He could comment on the relative merits of jails, some of which "would stink like that one" in Fort Worth, or have bunks like "that one in Portsmouth, just a plank with bedbugs in the cracks."

He met an old man who was a backslid Baptist preacher, a person who also found a place in Anderson's first novel, a personage of a type that Steinbeck would later mold into a major character for *Grapes of Wrath*. Anderson called the old hobo "Dad" in his novel and recounts that Dad had deserted a promiscuous wife and taken to the road, carrying with him plans for a "humming-bird airplane," which he had shown "in Lindbergh's office in New York, he said." The only thing holding the old inventor back was his lack of "twenty-five dollars to have a model made."

It was to be Acel Stecker, however, whom Anderson makes do the preaching in *Hungry Men* when these two are brought together:

> I've been thinking that if the preachers quit yelping about hell and pro-hibition and dancing," Acel said, "and took an interest in things that mat-tered, they would come a lot nearer emulating Jesus Christ. Why don't they drive out a few money lenders? They holler, 'Give to the poor,' but they don't realize that there is no need for the poor at all.

The old man replies, "I haven't preached in twelve years."

In his notes, and even more so in his mind, Anderson stored up hundreds of vivid scenes and characters: hoboes in ragged trousers and busted-out shoes, seedy small-town cops with their bellies hanging over their gunbelts, poor girls with their ideas of love fluctuating uncertainly between what they saw on the screen at the Bijou and what they heard through thin apartment walls at night. Anderson's main scene, however, was always the hobo jungle, a clearing in some scrub oaks just a stone's throw from a railroad. Blackened cans and empty rubbing alcohol bottles strewn both the ground and the bank of the gully in which a creek ran. A dozen hoboes occupied the little clearing, one shaving with "a mirror fixed in the bark of a tree," another "naked to the waist" and climbing up the bank with a can of water, a third lying "on a spread of newspapers with his head wrapped up in a coat." Hardly the setting of a Jane Austen novel, but in its way this curious half world had a distinctive culture and code of con-duct that Anderson had learned thoroughly by the time he arrived back in Abilene in 1933.

Things were looking up by the time Anderson rolled back into his hometown toward the end of that year. In March, the very month Franklin D. Roosevelt took office, something else had happened that would affect Anderson's future: Martha Foley and Whit Burnett, bringing from Europe their new magazine called *Story,* saw the first edition through the press, an edition carrying an April dateline. April was the month that Anderson had begun seriously collecting material for what was to become his first novel. He had begun by jumping ship in New Orleans in April, and through the spring and summer he con-tinued to make notes on the life of a Depression hobo. Roosevelt's New Dealers had a dozen schemes going to put some ginger back into the economy, but Anderson didn't look for any leaf-raking jobs when he hit Abilene that fall. Once he had said hello to his folks, Anderson looked up his friend John Knox to show him his sackful of manuscript notes. "I recognized some very rich and meaty stuff, and encouraged him to organize it," Knox later recalled.

Back in his little garage apartment, Anderson put a new ribbon on his upright typewriter and began hammering out some sketches. One, called "Bare Legs," was the story of a woman hoboing with her husband. She despises her husband as a weakling, trifles with another tramp, and sadly discovers that her husband has more spine than she suspects. Another, called "The Guy in the Blue Overcoat," concerned a twenty-three-year-old hobo and an even younger hobo called "the Kid." Trouble comes when the older bum tries to panhandle a couple of onions to go with two bits' worth of grub.

The hobo novel that Anderson finally wrote has Acel Stecker speculating as to whether a thirsty hobo hidden in "a reefer," or refrigerator car, could be the basis of literature. "It would make a short story, one of those short short stories they print in *Liberty,*" thinks Anderson's alter ego. "Writers got one hundred dollars for those stories." Anderson would try *Liberty, Saturday Evening Post,* and other high-paying markets first with his hobo yarns, but the stories eventually found a home with *Story,* for a good deal more prestige and a good deal less money. At the time it would seem to Anderson like a bad break. *Story* paid twenty-five dollars per piece.

His main project, however, was the novel. In November, when he had it in a shape that satisfied him, Anderson wrote Melba in Houston that it had taken him seven months to get it together. Anderson showed a draft to Knox, who looked at it with interest and "found much good in it." Knox's experience and wide reading made him constructively critical. "I told him he needed a stronger thread on which to string his beads—not a plot, as I used them in formula stories, but some motive, aim, goal, for his protagonist." Houston Heitchew agreed with that assessment and noted some other details needing work.

Anderson went back to his garage apartment, rolled himself a cigarette, lit it, and settled back in tobacco-induced tranquillity to mull over the problem. Make Acel a prizefighter? One minor bout in the ring had not taught Anderson enough about the business. A newspaper reporter? There were too many books about the news racket already. Through the smoke, he focused on his old trombone in the corner of the little room. So Acel Stecker became an out-of-work musician. "It has been two years since I played in that Juarez cabaret.

Godamighty," thinks Stecker in the second chapter. "I thought I was too good for that Spick's orchestra in Juarez, and that's why he fired me." Stecker believed his musicianship several notches above the others' because he had "played in a lot better bands."

Stecker's career in music parallels Anderson's career in journalism fairly well. While half-listening to a lowbrow Dale Carnegie philosopher during a thumbed ride, Stecker rehearses the job pitch he plans to make in New York: "It was like this, Mr. Gholson, I didn't know times were going to be so hard, so I quit the Apaches and with a few hundred I'd saved worked my way to Europe." Toward the end of the novel, Stecker teams up with two musician hoboes named Lou and Wayne to form a street band. This turn of events provides the book, although it is essentially open-ended, with a feeling of culmination.

Anderson, listening to the advice of Knox and Heitchew, provided his picaresque story with many of the elements of the traditional novel. Anderson managed to include a boy-meets-girl love story, for instance, although there is little nineteenth-century, Harold Bell Wright sentimentality about it. In the middle of the novel, Acel Stecker meets the unemployed New York typist named Corinne, "A slender girl with a grey tunic coat on her arm. . . . A pancake hat tilted forward over her right eye. She had a long nose and a dark complexion." Their courting speeches are flat and naturalistic: "No kiddin', sweet, I'm beginning to feel sorry I met you. I was getting along pretty good without a girl, and then one like you comes along and makes me wish I had one. I'm sorry I met you, because now I'll think about you. That's the trouble with you, honey, you're too sweet."

Corinne manages to reply, "You are sweet yourself." Stecker rises only to such poetry as "I'm gettin' fogbound over you," and his way of pressing his suit on Corinne lacks subtlety:

"You had much experience, honey?"

"Sure."

"I mean, you know the kind of experience I mean?"

"Sure."

"I mean sex experience."

"Sure."

Soon the pair are living together, Acel vending razor blades on the streets, Corinne selling classified ads. Then Stecker gets into trouble with the police and has to hit the road, promising without any real hope to send for Corinne later.

When Anderson finally hacked out the last revised page, the book still lacked a title. Where should he go for a name? Perhaps to the Bible, as Robert Cantwell would later do for *Land of Plenty*, Steinbeck for *Grapes of Wrath*, James Agee for *Let Us Now Praise Famous Men* (all of which are famous Depression books written after Anderson's 1933 novel). Perhaps he should go to his imagination, as Edward Dahlberg had for *Bottom Dogs*, as Hemingway would for *To Have and Have Not*. John Knox suggested he go back to Knut Hamsun. The first great success of Hamsun had been *Sult* (in English, *Hunger*). Knox suggested he vary that to *Hungry Men*.

6. Love and Votes

‑‑ ‑‑

One April morning shortly after Easter in 1934, a pretty girl named Polly Anne Bates walked with her friend Dora Fallon down the high-ceilinged hallway of the Administration Building at McMurry College in Abilene. Between classes the hall was crowded, although not as crowded as it would have been a few years previously, before the Depression had cut into enrollment. McMurry in 1934 had fewer than three-hundred students.

Dora Fallon carried a notebook and a textbook. She was an English major, and she was going to an English class taught by Professor Julia Luker. Dora was a round-faced girl with serious eyes under her short, slicked-down hair. She was chubby.

Polly Anne Bates had brown hair and lively green eyes, striking eyes that caused friends to compare her appearance with that of actress Sylvia Sidney. She was 5'5" tall, with a graceful 120-pound figure. She was obviously quite young, only eighteen in fact. She carried no books, because she wasn't a regular student.

Polly Anne Bates knew her way around McMurry College, however, because she took private lessons from the college's art teacher, Ruby McIntosh. To reach Professor McIntosh's studio Polly Anne regularly climbed the Administration Building stairs past the nine-thousand-volume college library on the second floor. Once she reached the third, the top floor, she walked past the science lab and the home economics department to the east end of the hall, where the fine arts department studios were. As a matter of fact, all the teaching that went on at McMurry took place in the Administration Building, and there were classrooms on all three floors.

Polly Anne was tagging along with Dora to English class that day because an Abilene writer and poet named John Knox was supposed to talk to Professor Luker's class.

The college had just emerged from a dark period of mourning. Dr. James Winfred Hunt, the founder of McMurry, had died only a month earlier, on March 12, finally free of the responsibilities and debts of his small, young college. Even before the Wall Street Crash, McMurry had sailed into choppy financial waters when enrollment dropped in the 1928–29 school year and the budget went twelve-thousand dollars into the red. Hunt had struggled with the increasingly heavy deficits for five more years, and this may have been a factor in his final illness. Dr. Hunt's body had lain in state in the small, classical auditorium in the center of the yellow-brick Administration Building, a structure Hunt had planted eleven years earlier on a bald stretch of prairie at the southern end of Abilene's streetcar line. Heavy, life-size oil paintings of Hunt and Bishop William Fletcher McMurry, for whom the college was named, hung on either side of the auditorium's stage. The Methodist bishop had died only weeks before Hunt.

The deaths of old men weigh lightly on the consciousness of the young. It was spring. Dora and Polly Anne, vaguely and excitedly conscious of the young men hurrying around them in the corridor, would speculate on whether the visiting poet would prove handsome and single.

Dora led Polly Anne into the large classroom, where they took seats near the front. Most of the seats were filled by the time Professor Luker rose to make the introduction. Luker was passionately interested in writing (and in her later years published an autobiographical novel, *The Yeoman's Daughter*). In her introduction, she pointed out that Knox was founding editor of the *Galleon*, McMurry's literary magazine; that he was once editor of the *Totem*, McMurry's yearbook; and that he was also a former sub-editor of the *War Whoop*, McMurry's newspaper — all of which Luker sponsored. Since leaving McMurry, Knox had published poetry in a number of magazines, and for a time had himself edited *Troubadour* and *Tom-Tom*, two poetry magazines.

Perhaps Mr. Knox will read us today something from his book of sonnets, *Through a Glass Darkly*. Mr. Knox has supported himself writing magazine fiction for the past two years. Accompanying Mr. Knox today is another writer. . . .

John Knox spread out on the lectern a sheaf of paper he had brought with him.

> Some men must walk with Hunger all their days
> And scorn the halls where easy feasts are spread;
> They must pass on through black, uncharted ways;
> And eat their souls . . .

Polly Anne glanced furtively at the accompanying writer, whom Luker had identified as Edward Anderson. He was a good four inches shorter than Knox, but lean and muscular. He had dark, wavy hair. Polly Anne thought him very handsome. He hadn't said a word.

>   . . . but never touch your bread.
> With halo, crown or ashes on your head,
> Go tempt them with the sweet food of a lie,
> And they will choose sharp rocks of doubt instead,
> And some shall starve, but some shall never die.

While all other eyes were on Knox, Anderson glanced around the class at the coeds. His attention did not linger long with Dora, but his gaze stopped on Polly Anne Bates, stopped longer than was really polite.

> Ah, madmen, who through wilderness and night
> Go hungry, and on bleeding feet pursue
> What men are pleased to call a phantom light,
> These lips shall never dare to laugh at you,
> Being afraid that for some piercing thorn
> A tomb may crack, a temple veil be torn!

When the girl with the Sylvia Sidney eyes went home for lunch that day, she was still turning the poems and the two young writers over in her mind. She had gone to the reading that morning because, although she, like her mother, painted, she was also interested in the other arts.

She was born Viola Lanham Bates on July 22, 1915, in Fort Worth, Texas, but her constant optimism early led her father to hang on her a nickname drawn from the optimistic heroine of Eleanor Porter's 1913 novel *Pollyanna.* Her mother, Pearl C. Jones, had been a schoolteacher before she married Polly Anne's father, L. E. Bates, a man always called "Dick" by his family and friends. Polly Anne was born into a family heavily engaged not in the arts but in law enforcement. One of Polly Anne's uncles was chief of police for San Angelo, Texas. He hired Dick Bates for the force there. The best-known lawman in the family was Gus T. Jones ("Uncle Bucky" to Polly Anne), who was first a Texas Ranger and later an FBI agent, playing a key role in the Urschel kidnaping case and the manhunt for John Dillinger; in the arrests of Harvey Bailey, Machine-Gun Kelly, and Albert Bates; in the end of Butch Cassidy and the Hole-in-the-Wall Gang. His adventures are told in George Ellis's book, *A Man Named Jones.*

Polly Anne's earliest memories were of her father in the uniform of a San Angelo policeman. Dick Bates later also became an FBI agent, what the newspapers of the thirties loved to call a G-man. Because the Justice Department moved its agents frequently, Polly. Anne (the youngest child, with an older twin brother and sister) saw a good deal of the state. In the mid-twenties, she saw the great John Philip Sousa conduct a concert in Houston. The musical taste of Dick Bates, like that of Edward Anderson, ran more to Jimmie Rodgers and "I'm in the Jailhouse Now." Dick Bates liked to settle down after supper now and then to play his harmonica with a couple of pals taking guitar and fiddle. Polly Anne, however, had listened to a teacher's recording of *Poet and Peasant* in the fourth grade and decided she preferred heavier music, Brahms and Puccini and their sort. "Shut off that noise," her father would sometimes protest. There were other small acts of rebellion, such as the time in high school when she got a panjola haircut, a fad in which the hair was short like a boy's, complete with faked sideburns. Little things, nothing important. Just enough for the Methodist church secretary in Abilene to jokingly call her "a bit of a nut."

One of the original FBI agents, Dick Bates was not pleased when J. Edgar Hoover, whom Bates called "just a clerk," was named head of the FBI in 1924. Bates hated all the reports and other paperwork that Hoover began requiring. Finally, after returning from Alaska and a troublesome case involving pirates who raided fishing boats, Bates was forced by bad health to retire. On December 16, 1930, his family celebrated his fifty-seventh birthday. Three days later, while puttering around in his backyard, Bates suffered a massive heart attack. Pearl Bates and Polly Anne somehow managed to get the 185-pound man up a flight of stairs and on a bed. It was no use. He was dead. The grief-stricken family faced a bleak Christmas. Polly Anne did not return to her high-school studies in the spring of 1931.

Bates had not had time to do so, but he had indicated that he wanted to move to Abilene after he retired. Pearl Bates and Polly Anne first visited an elderly aunt in Abilene and then in 1932 moved there. Pearl's older daughter, by then married, already lived in Abilene, and the twin brother went to work at an Abilene service station. Mrs. Bates became very active in the First Methodist Church, and Polly Anne followed along.

Soon after the April, 1934, poetry reading, Edward Anderson was catching up on his reading at the Carnegie Library. In the periodicals section, the newspapers were full of stories about the bandit lovers, Bonnie and Clyde. On Easter Sunday the Barrow gang had gunned down Texas highway patrolmen E. B. Wheeler and H. B. Murphy at Grapevine, just outside of Dallas. Everyone knew what Bonnie and Clyde looked like, and when a few days later Bonnie entered a drugstore in Texarkana, the cashier and soda jerk tried not to stare. Clyde and their driver, Henry Methvin, had remained outside, but they became suspicious and one of them went inside to fetch her. Bonnie left her sandwich, half eaten, on the counter. The fugitives ate cold beans hurriedly bought at roadside groceries and slept in hasty camps or in their car. Another April day the Barrow car got stuck on a muddy road near Miami, Oklahoma; when two local cops came out to investigate, the Barrows killed one and kidnaped the other. So April went. Dark and bloody business, bad for Bonnie and Clyde. Good material for a novel if anyone was smart enough to see it.

Anderson heard the door open and glanced up to see the green-eyed girl from the poetry reading. She turned in her books at the desk and began browsing the shelves. What kind of book, Anderson would wonder, was she looking for? Maybe *Anthony Adverse,* which had already sold more than 300,000 copies; Harvey Allen had constructed a 1,224-page time machine to whisk Americans away from the Depression. Maybe *So Red the Rose* by Stark Young, or *Good-bye, Mr. Chips* by James Hilton, all of them current best-sellers. Certainly not *God's Little Acre* by Erskine Caldwell or *The Young Manhood of Studs Lonigan* by James Farrell; if Maude E. Cole had acquired either, she would have it under lock and key. The green-eyed girl glanced quickly past the complete multivolume set of Sir James George Frazer's *Golden Bough* and another matched set containing the complete works of Tasso, Aretino, and other Italians. Some bawdy stuff there, but in that lofty style unlikely to corrupt the youth of Abilene. Had anyone besides John H. Knox and Houston Heitchew ever disturbed them? The green

Polly Anne Bates

eyes barely glanced at the gold-stamped names on the dusty spines.

Anderson watched her with interest. Young but in high heels, to him a sign of maturity. Hair cut short (but no longer in a panjola). Skirt longer than it would have been ten years before, but still short enough to reveal two well-shaped legs. A high-waisted dress, frilly at the bosom. Just the hint of a smile on her red lips, as though she knew something but wasn't telling. A hat that rose high over her left eye and made an impudent plunge over her right.

She checked out more books and started to leave. Anderson, on an impulse, got up and rushed to follow her to the door. He caught her outside, on the steps.

Hey, wait a minute.

In the library she had seen, out of the corner of her eye, the handsome young writer who had been with John Knox in Professor Luker's classroom. Now she couldn't bring herself to look directly at him. He grasped her shyness from the way she kept her eyes down, looking at the square concrete planters flanking the entrance.

Hello. He was Edward Anderson, and wasn't she in the class at McMurry that he visited recently?

Yes. Only she wasn't exactly in the class. She had been visiting too.

What was her name?

Bates. Polly Anne Bates.

They talked, Anderson self-assured as always with a woman, Polly Anne hesitant and yet flattered by the attention of an older man, a genuine writer, a man of the world. She showed him the titles of the books she had chosen.

He had been reading a little, taking a break from working.

Working?

On a story, about his travels as a hobo.

This was more like it. Far from the Parisian Left Bank, far even from Mabel Dodge's Taos, Polly heard little talk about the arts.

Suddenly he asked her for a date. For Sunday.

Oh, she couldn't. She would have to go to church. Mother likes her to go to church.

Why doesn't he see her at church? Which church?

The First Methodist Church.

Oh, he knew that one. He had played his trombone there on a program.

Polly had never heard anyone play trombone in the First Methodist Church, or even heard secondhand of such a thing. She didn't say no, however.

Pearl Bates did not drive. When Sunday evening came, Polly backed out the big gray Buick, with her mother in the passenger seat, and steered off toward Butternut Street where the red-brick First Method-

ist Church stood facing east. As with so many Methodist church buildings of that era, its main entrance was at the top of a steep flight of
stairs worthy of an ancient temple in a Cecil B. DeMille motion picture. A half century later, a Methodist minister would note that "a
lot of people who built those churches can't hobble up the steps to
get in them today."

Edward Anderson was waiting outside. Since he wanted to create
the best possible first impression, he wore a suit, a necktie, even a
hat, which was an item he normally put on for only the ritziest occasions. Polly, in her best dress, her lips newly reddened, her green eyes
sparkling, saw him. She introduced Mrs. Bates, who lingered a moment and then went up the majestic flight of steps. Polly and Edward
entered, a young man and young woman dressed in their best. The
Sunday evening service was relatively informal, but these two had
plumed themselves for one another rather than for the brothers and
sisters of the church. They sat down in a pew, not too close to one
another, conscious of every inch of proximity.

The congregation began a hymn. Mrs. Bates glanced over to re-
assure herself that Polly was there. A prayer, another hymn. Then the
Reverend W. C. Childress, a man of medium height with black curly
hair and gray eyes, stood up to talk. None of that fiery oratory common to so many southern preachers' sermons. Along with one of the
Gospels, he quoted Harry Emerson Fosdick. Polly whispered to Edward that Childress had eight children.

A collection plate. More singing. A prayer. With relief, the young
couple finally got back outside, where a friendly darkness let them
look directly at one another, let them talk a little. Around them the
scattering Methodists smiled, exchanged final trivialities, got into
cars, and started them.

Edward said that he would call Polly.

Mrs. Bates came down the steps, observant, careful to look pleasant. She stood a little away from the two as Polly said good-night.
Anderson watched them, mother and daughter, get into the Buick
and drive away.

One evening in May, Edward arrived on foot at 1318 Jeanette. On
a beautiful night in West Texas, when the farmers are clamoring for
rain, skies hang over the town with a blue purity that makes you feel
you might reach up and pull down a handful of stars. Polly answered
his knock at the door.

Where did he want to go?

He didn't know. Over to his place?

Edward and Polly came outside just four years too late to catch the last Abilene streetcar. They walked along the sidewalk, hand in hand, getting glimpses of the sky through the trees that lined Sayles Boulevard, trees acutely appreciated in this region of bald prairielands. Sayles was the prettiest thoroughfare in the city. Abilene's more successful merchants and ranchers had built their homes, many of them quite elaborate, along Sayles. These homeowners saw to it that the city cared for the trees down the boulevard's central islands, and the police were almost more likely to prosecute a man for driving his car into one of their trunks than for shooting an unfaithful wife.

Strolling north along Sayles, lingering, talking—for the walk was an end in itself—Edward and Anne took some time to go the thirteen blocks to North and South First streets, which run on each side of the Texas and Pacific Railroad. The tracks split Abilene in half; the phrase "from the other side of the tracks" has no shady connotation in Abilene. Sayles Boulevard, however, metamorphosed into a simple residential street, Graham, on the north side of North First. Edward and Anne walked three more blocks on Graham to the Anderson home. A delightful trip, but a long one on foot, a mile and a half. Fortunately, Polly was quite young, and Edward was a man who walked tirelessly and enjoyed walking all his days.

They turned at the driveway before they got to the house and went directly to the little red-brick garage apartment. He flipped the switch to cut away the darkness, and she walked over to examine the title of a book on the writing table: *Pan* by Knut Hamsun. She reminded him that he had promised to show her the manuscript of his own novel to her.

Was she sure she wanted to see it?

Yes, of course.

Edward hauled it out and warned her to be gentle with it; manuscripts get worn quickly enough traveling from publisher to publisher. Polly fastened her green eyes on it and leafed through the first few pages without being able to concentrate enough to make any sense out of them.

Edward moved to stand beside her.

She put the manuscript down. There was an odd apparatus over there. What was it?

He told her that it was a machine for rolling cigarettes. He would teach her to roll cigarettes for him.

There was a knock at the door.

Who was it?

Louise, his sister. They needed the cigarette roller in the house. Oh, all right. She could come in and get it.

Polly felt it was time she started for home anyway.

Was she sure she'd rested enough? Well, he would walk her back now.

Early on the morning of May 23, 1934, Clyde Barrow and Bonnie Parker discovered the truck belonging to Irvin Methvin, father of fellow bandit Henry Methvin, jacked up and with the right wheel removed. It stood beside the road, eight miles out of Gibsland, Louisiana. Clyde, who was driving, slowed down so that he and Bonnie could scout the situation. Halt! It was a trap. Clyde tried to run for it. A barrage of gunfire killed the slender bandit and his pretty, blond paramour.

Many of Edward and Polly's dates continued to be walking dates. Edward's mother had taken a strong dislike to Polly the one time the girl entered the red-brick house on Graham; Mrs. Anderson was in no mood to lend the family car. So up and down Sayles they walked. Some first-rate motion pictures came out that year — Fred and Ginger danced their way to stardom in *Flying Down to Rio,* Leslie Howard played a character learning about life in Maugham's *Of Human Bondage* — but Edward had very little money to spare, and he had never been much of a movie-goer. Soda fountains were in their heyday; it was no accident that most of the big scenes in Carl Ed's widely read "Harold Teen" comic strip took place in Poppa Jenks's Sugar Bowl. Edward and Polly frequented the fountain at Linton's Drug Store on North Second and Pine, which wasn't far from the Carnegie Library. Or they sipped nickel coffees in a cafe. Songwriters Billy Rose and Al Dubin had recently transformed Omar Khayyám's "jug of wine, a loaf of bread, and thou" into "a cup of coffee, a sandwich, and you" for a scrap of melody by Joe Meyer. But mostly Polly and Edward walked back and forth on Sayles, and Polly read Edward's manuscript — and she learned to manufacture cigarettes on the cigarette-rolling machine.

John and Mabel Knox came through town one day. Since John was not living in Abilene at the time, Polly had not seen him since the fateful poetry reading at McMurry. Edward and Polly hosted John and Mabel in the tight confines of the little garage apartment.

Knox, as was usual with him in those days, had some booze with him. Taylor County, of which Abilene is the seat, had voted dry twice in the year that followed the repeal of Prohibition in 1933. As a treat, Knox dragged out his bottle and poured four whiskeys, one for each of the group. The talk went on. Literature. Books. More literature. Knox noticed that, while Edward and Mabel were sipping with enjoyment, Polly nursed her drink sheepishly. She had never tasted the foul stuff before, obviously. Knox gulped down his drink. Then in a low-key act calculated to save Polly any embarrassment, Knox reached over and lifted away Polly's glass. "Here, I'll take that." He continued to talk while drinking her whiskey also. Polly was greatly relieved. She always remembered the chivalrous act. "I knew that here was a true gentleman, a very kind man."

Anderson had seldom stayed in one place long enough to establish residence and vote. Like many journalists, however, he watched politics with an interest tinged with cynicism. Then in 1934 he plunged into the whirlpool of a Texas political campaign. The reason was money. Max Bentley remembered Edward when he heard that a Dallas lawyer named William McCraw was going to run for Texas attorney general and wanted to hire a good man as publicist and general gofer — such genteel terms as "public relations" had not really spread much beyond Madison Avenue in those days. Edward snagged the job. For the first time in four years Edward had a decently salaried, if temporary, berth. Its worst drawback was that it took Edward out of Abilene in the middle of his courtship of Polly Anne Bates.

Every voter in Texas was being courted by McCraw, thirty-seven years old, red-headed, getting a little paunchy. Like Anderson, McCraw grew up in a print shop, his father's in Dallas, and he started out working as a printer's devil and selling newspapers. Then at nineteen, he passed the state's bar examination to become one of the youngest attorneys in Texas; his disabilities as a minor had to be removed by court action so that he could practice.

When the United States entered World War I, McCraw went through officers' training and was commissioned a second lieutenant in the cavalry. Since by then the War Department had realized there was no place for do-or-die horsemen in the grisly, barbed-wire-hedged no-man's-land of Europe, McCraw was transferred to the 132nd Machine Gun Brigade and shipped to France with Texas' 36th "Arrow-head" Division. After the Armistice, McCraw returned to Dallas to hang out his shingle again. He tried public office as an assistant district attorney, and liking it, he ran for criminal district attorney. Dallas voters elected him in 1926, 1928, and 1930.

Texas voters are scattered over a vast area, and McCraw in 1934 covered as much of it as was humanly possible in his Cadillac. With Anderson driving. Edward got back to Abilene to see Polly only sporadically. After hammering out press releases on his portable typewriter, he frequently composed letters to her full of political anecdotes. He told Polly about how they would roll into a tank town and stop to allow McCraw to get out and press flesh with the voters around the square. They had a loudspeaker hooked up to a phonograph mounted on top of the car. One day as it played "Lady of Spain," Anderson noticed that McCraw, bone tired but with a big smile locked into his jaws, was shaking hands in exact tempo with the music of the popular waltz. On another occasion, weary and driving at night, Anderson had taken his eyes off the road to touch the automobile's glowing lighter to the tip of his cigarette. The Cadillac left the road and hit a culvert. The impact threw Anderson out the door, but fortunately he escaped any injuries more serious than scratches, bruises, and torn clothing.

In his speeches, McCraw boasted of his tough record as Dallas district attorney, boasted that he had set a new national record for ninety-nine-year sentences given for robbery, boasted that in 1927 he had persuaded juries and judges to give twenty-six hundred years in sentences, boasted that in 1928 there had been only ten acquittals among 272 cases tried.

Anderson cranked out press releases about his blameless home life. McCraw was married to the former Louise Britton, "who was a popular Theta at the University of Texas." At the latest possible moment, McCraw left the campaign trail to return to Louise at their suburban home northwest of Dallas, a home where a pre-election profile story said they raised "chickens and ducks and garden truck, and take great pride in fine Bermuda onions, peas, beans and tomatos."

Bill and Louise, Edward and Polly awaited the verdict of the people. When it came, the *Abilene Reporter-News* called it "the upset of the day." The following morning, Sunday, July 29, Texas Election Bureau figures showed McCraw led his two opponents by a healthy margin, although he still faced a runoff. McCraw had 155,968 votes, a total well ahead of a West Texas senator named Walter C. Woodward, who had 142,422. Clyde E. Smith of Tyler trailed at third with 78,225.

Toward the end of the runoff race between McCraw and Woodward, Edward and Polly decided to get married. The opposition of both the Anderson and Bates families pushed them toward a decision. In addition to Ellen Anderson's having developed an instant aversion to Polly, E. H. had concerns about his son's courting a girl Polly's age. Edward vaguely assured him that Polly could take care of herself. The Anderson daughters varied in attitude. Dorothy, who at twenty was closest to Polly's age, got along best with her, and Polly used to walk down Sayles to share Edward's campaign-trail letters with Dorothy.

Over at the Bates house on Jeanette Street, Pearl was even more worried about her daughter, who was barely nineteen. Mrs. Bates had immersed Polly in activities at the First Methodist Church in the hope that she would meet a solid young Methodist man. Edward did not seem the sort to regularly attend Wesleyan prayer meetings. Her son, L. E., Jr., had turned the heavily muscular body he inherited not to law enforcement like so many other men in the family but rather to auto mechanics, yet L. E. had begun intimating that he might have to do something about this guy sparking Polly.

On the Wednesday before the election Edward was back in Abilene from campaigning. Over sodas at a table in Jack Linton's drugstore, Edward sensed that the girl with the Sylvia Sidney eyes was troubled. What was it? Polly admitted it was her brother. The men in her family were no strangers to the use of lethal weapons.

Edward was a man of decision. Let's get married. None of this going-down-on-one-knee stuff.

A doctor's office was just a few steps away for a blood test. The county courthouse was only a couple of blocks south of the T&P tracks. They told no one. On that August Saturday, election day, Edward found an excuse to take the Anderson family car. He drove down Sayles for a change and picked up Polly. They drove to the parsonage of the First Presbyterian Church, where Edward had first met John five years previously. John, himself now settled in a marriage that found scant approval with his parents, was not there. The Reverend Dr. T. S. Knox came to the door when Edward knocked. Edward and Polly explained that they wanted him to marry them.

There were no members of their families present. Were they sure? Wouldn't they like to get in touch with their families, talk about it, have some of them present? The scholarly old minister liked Edward, and he knew firsthand the pain that parents experienced in these hasty matches.

"If you won't marry us, we'll go find someone who will."

Very well. Dr. Knox called in his wife, Lucille, and one of his daughters to serve as witnesses.

That same night, just twenty-nine days after their own third wedding anniversary, Bill and Louise McCraw again settled down in front of the radio in the living room of their home northwest of Dallas to await returns. They had to wait a while, but eventually McCraw began drawing ahead. The Sunday morning newspaper gave McCraw a hard-won 251,737 to 242,312 victory.

McCraw would serve two terms as Texas attorney general, leading many to think he would have the advantage when he announced for governor in 1938. But a new and unpredictable element entered Texas politics that year, a candidate named W. Lee O'Daniel, who had made himself known to most Texans by hawking Light Crust Flour over a powerful Texas radio station. Pappy O'Daniel took his Light Crust Doughboys string band out campaigning and beat all twelve of his opponents in the first primary in 1938. He topped their combined vote by 30,000. McCraw ran third.

McCraw's former publicist and his wife had left Texas by the 1938 election. It took the business they began on August 25, 1934, somewhat longer to run its course.

7. Writing Crime
in the Crescent City

So at age twenty-nine Edward had acquired a wife. Why now, after having been in love so many times since high school? Perhaps he was like his father, who, after several years as a playboy, had married at twenty-seven and settled down to raise a family. Of course, if Edward was unconsciously following in his father's footsteps, he was two years behind schedule, but the Depression had put everyone's timetable out of joint. E. H. had settled into the life of a printer after he married Ellen, but the life of a fiction writer is a lot quirkier than the routine of a print shop.

What sort of bride had Edward won? This green-eyed girl had a mind of her own. Although she had impressed the Methodist church secretary as being "scatterbrained," John Knox would look more closely and call her "bright and spunky." Ten years younger than her husband, she began by thinking Edward knew everything. That couldn't last. Edward would later employ the lament that "no man is a hero to his valet or his wife." At the time they exchanged vows, neither Edward nor Polly recognized a latent element in her character: she was, to use her own term, a "nest builder." She wanted children and a solid home in which to bring them up.

Both the Anderson and Bates families were rocked by the news of the marriage. Neither had any alternative but to adjust as best they could.

Mrs. Bates offered her daughter and new son-in-law the choice of a new set of silverware or one hundred dollars cash.

Without hesitation they took the cash.

Using that as a stake, Edward and Anne packed up their clothes, said their good-byes, and caught the bus out of Abilene. Bound for

New Orleans. Leaving West Texas to broil in dry and dusty heat, Edward and Anne would establish themselves during those last days of the 1934 summer in sultry, romantic New Orleans. She was Anne now, no longer Polly or Polly Anne; the new Mrs. Anderson felt that "Polly" sounded too immature for a matron with a literary husband. As for Mr. Anderson, who had been Andy in Houston and Eddie in Abilene, he would remain Edward to Anne, through thick and thin. "I never called him Eddie," she would say a half century later.

That year, 1934, was the year movie audiences first got to see Frank Capra's classic romantic comedy, *It Happened One Night,* with Claudette Colbert as a runaway heiress and Clark Gable as a tough-talking, hard-drinking reporter. There is a wonderful scene that takes place on a bus, with the heiress and reporter snapping at each other, although they are really just making the first moves in the mating game. Ward Bond is the bus driver, a heart of gold beneath a bulldog face. Somebody has a squeezebox, and all the passengers join together to sing "The Daring Young Man on the Flying Trapeze." Anne Anderson was not exactly a runaway or an heiress, just a pretty nineteen-year-old bride with her mama's hundred dollars. Edward Anderson, minus the Gable mustache, came a lot closer to being that tough-talking, hard-drinking reporter. Anne and Edward didn't argue; nobody can recall whether the bus driver looked like Ward Bond; almost certainly the passengers didn't join together in song. But the design of the bus, the style of the women's clothes, the cut of the men's suits, the atmosphere of the Depression thirties conveyed in Capra's wonderful bus trip provide good pictures of what the honeymoon trip must have looked like.

From Abilene to New Orleans, Anne and Edward rode seven hundred miles by bus. Anne was quite happy. Perhaps she sensed that she was about to begin the best year of her life. When the bus arrived at the broad Mississippi, a ferryboat took the newlyweds across to New Orleans. This was the Southern city with the deepest literary heritage, the city of Lafcadio Hearn and George Washington Cable. Less than a decade earlier, Sherwood Anderson and William Faulkner had ambled together down its narrow, Old World streets.

The first thing Edward did was to lead Anne into a bar and order two whiskeys. He drank his. She left hers. She was already intoxicated by the sight of the French Quarter. Edward, who had been to New Orleans before, enjoyed showing her this curious city, both South-

Newlyweds Edward and Anne in New Orleans

ern and cosmopolitan, with its half million inhabitants compounded
of French, Spanish, English, and African cultures.

"I like New Orleans," Edward had written in *Hungry Men,* in one
of the few places in the novel where he abandoned the third person
for the first. "It's kind of like a girl you have met two or three times
and didn't think so much of and then all of a sudden you see her
again and want to hold her."

Anne didn't wait for the second or third time; she fell in love with
the place at first glance. The lovers spent days just walking around,
getting familiar with the streets, looking in the windows of little grocery
stores that stocked big, garlicked olives and imported Swiss cheese,
touching the old iron grillwork that barred the street from the shady
cool of courtyard gardens, examining buildings that were more than
a century old when Dallas was founded and Abilene just another patch
of prairie in the vast empire of the Comanche Indians.

They settled down in the French Quarter, where the flavor of a
decayed civilization was more genuine in the thirties. At the corner
of St. Philip and Bourbon streets stood the old Lafitte Hotel, where
they rented a large second-floor room with a balcony that ran the
length of the room. If they shared the bathroom at the end of the
hall with other guests, well, that was part of the charm.

Mornings, when the sky had hardly shed its pink for daytime blue,
Anne would get up before Edward, before most of the worldly wise
New Orleanians, and go down to the docks on the Mississippi to
watch the dockhands unloading the banana boats. From there she
could see the new Huey P. Long Bridge, almost four and a half miles
long, a thirteen-million-dollar eighth wonder of the world allowing
automobiles to drive across the broad Mississippi where once drivers
had had to pay fare on a ferry.

Then Anne would buy hot coffee and hot rolls. She would take
them back to the Lafitte, where Edward would have awakened by then
and be shaving, thinking out his day.

In the late afternoons, Anne found music in the steam whistles of
the peanut vendors, whistles that could be heard blocks away. With
an artist's eye, she watched a little child, four or five years old, clutch-
ing a lard pail filled with beer in one hand, holding three tailor-made
cigarettes in the other, carrying them back to a father or mother ready
to relax after a hard day's work. In the evenings, Edward took her
to the little bars where small jazz bands blew hot and blue—"High

Society," "Beale Street Blues," "Goodbye to Storyville"—in the great tradition that had its birth in the city's red-light district back before World War I. The customers tossed money into a big kitty for the musicians. On such excursions, Edward generally drank beer and Anne drank Dr. Pepper.

Anne was entranced by Jackson Square, that lovely little park bounded by Chartres, St. Peter, St. Ann, and Decatur streets. Most days she found an excuse to go by there, to rest on a park bench, to study the shape of St. Louis Cathedral and the play of light and shadow on it. She soon sketched it, the first sketch Anne did in New Orleans.

One hundred dollars was a lot of money in 1934. In the days when you could dine on a blue-plate special for a quarter and buy a man's business suit for twelve bucks, a "century note" would purchase ten times as much as the same amount would purchase a half century later. Yet even a reservoir of one hundred 1934 dollars would eventually go dry.

Edward realized this, although Anne was still too starry-eyed to care. He turned to crime. But only as an observer. He had sold one case history to a true detective magazine back when he had begun experimenting with writing something besides newspaper journalism. He looked around him for material. A check with the files of local newspapers showed that New Orleans, like most old cities with a lot of poor at the bottom of the economic pyramid, had plenty of larceny and homicide. To his delight, Anderson also discovered that the magazines had scarcely noticed even the most lurid New Orleans murders. Perhaps they hadn't had the time; true detective magazines were relatively new.

Bernarr Macfadden had created *True Detective Mysteries* in 1924 to see if readers would be interested in the real thing as much as they were in the avalanche of fictional sleuthing of that era. It clicked, although it succeeded more modestly than the naughty confessions that began in Macfadden's *True Story* in 1919. *True Detective* bred a host of imitators, including another Macfadden publication, *Master Detective.* Everywhere newsstands displayed the cover photographs of buxom females, scantily clad, hands tied, screaming when menaced by some thug wielding a Turkish dagger, corkscrew, buzz saw, or even more bizarre murder weapon. The detectives sold well, attracted many pages of advertising, and paid authors respectable amounts.

Anderson mailed off several proposals to editors and got some encouraging nibbles at his bait. Soon he was selling steadily: "Undercovering the Vice Cesspool in New Orleans: The Shameful Facts behind the War between T. Semmes (Turkeyhead) Walmsely and Huey (Kingfish) Long," "Tough Guy! The Career of Dutch Gardner," "The Mystery of the Man with the Cardboard Box," "The Kiss of Death and New Orleans' Diamond Queen." The best market, the magazine with the highest reputation, was *True Detective,* which required an affidavit from a peace officer attesting to the truth of the manuscript. Anderson tried them first, and sold *True Detective* such titles as "New Orleans' Twin Trunk Murders," "The Strange Killing of Diamond Kate," and "The Black Cat—and the Four Who Hanged."

Edward wrote an article devoted to Henry Meyer, the official hangman for the state of Louisiana. He and Anne were fascinated by this curious old character who held a position at once sinister and surrounded by romantic legend, oddly different from the lawmen in Anne's family. Old Henry was said to get "skunk drunk" after an execution.

In his *True Detective* story "The Black Cat—and the Four Who Hanged," Anderson ended with the sentence: "The execution required only seventy minutes, and technically speaking, was a good job for Henry Meyer, the hangman." The old man told Anne and Edward about his very first hanging. When he was a child, his pet dog had become ill. He had taken it up on the roof, put a rope around its neck, and pushed it off.

By early 1935, Edward knew that Anne had their first child in the making, so he took a newspaper job on the desk of the *New Orleans States* to provide an income more stable than was possible freelancing. With much of his time now demanded by his job, Edward suggested Anne try her hand at collecting material for his true detective pieces. She did for a time. He did not bother to mention that he had somehow gotten crosswise with the New Orleans police, a fact she did not learn until many years later. She gathered the facts during his working hours, and he sat down at the portable borrowed from his sister Dorothy to whack out the magazine stories in his off time.

"I'll never forget one time I was going up the steps to talk to the police," Anne said. "The jail was up above, and I looked up to see a convicted murderer, a man named Kenneth Neu, who was to be executed in a few days—and he was standing in the window of his cell singing 'Blue Moon.'" To the haunting Richard Rodgers melody, Neu sang Lorenz Hart's words about being left all alone and without dreams.

"That was almost too much for somebody like me," Anne said. "I almost didn't make it up the steps."

In New Orleans, artist Karl Sherman became the current friend of Edward, as John Knox had been in Abilene. Somehow Anderson still couldn't take the next step, from having just one friend to having many friends. Karl Sherman was from Philadelphia, and he was in New Orleans to do enough oil paintings, watercolors, and drawings for a one-man show. The Andersons met him in the French Quarter. Over friendly beers in the evenings, Sherman told them how he had come from Russia to America in steerage in 1911, how the first-class passengers on the upper deck had thrown down bananas and chocolates, delicacies the eight-year-old Karl had never tasted, and how he had known they were leaving his grandmother in Russia to starve. For a few years he had been a resident of the Hebrew Orphans Home in Philadelphia. He had later dropped out of high school to work in a sheet-metal shop. But he had an artist's hands, an artist's eye for the world; so Sherman studied at the Fleischer Memorial Art School, a free school situated at Seventh and Catherine streets in Philadelphia. His work had previously won him a scholarship to the Philadelphia Academy of Fine Arts, but, unhappy with the academy's teaching methods, Sherman had dropped out.

Since she herself painted, Anne was particularly fascinated. Sherman employed a high-keyed palette. His pictures were almost without human subjects; the single exception was *Joseph*, a study of a black youth. Sherman preferred the old walls of the French Quarter, and put them on canvas dripping with color. He liked the quaint dilapidation of courtyards, and the tilt of balconies. His *Airway — French Quarter* showed a balcony perilously pitched over a narrow passageway, while balconies at various angles hung over a courtyard in Chartres Street. There were balconies rounding corners and other architectural features that suggested the French influence in the city. A bird cage against an old stucco wall could have been in Paris. Sherman painted long red buildings, garden corners, the boats of many nations in the harbor, great live oaks, Jackson Square with its equestrian statue.

Critics in New Orleans liked his work, but the reception for his one-man show later in Philadelphia would not be so good. Neverthe-

Caricature of Edward by Karl Sherman

less, in Philadelphia he would stay, eventually joining the faculty of Philadelphia College of Fine Art.

After his return to the East, Sherman would write Edward and Anne from time to time, but Edward never answered, as was his practice. Sherman remained very much with the Andersons, however, by way of two likenesses he sketched of Edward, one a better-than-photographic pencil drawing of the writer's face at three-quarters angle, the other a caricature in which a few simple lines were rich in suggestion of character.

Magazines providing a large number of readers for serious fiction were scarce in the thirties, and in fact have been scarce during most of the twentieth century. It was Edward Anderson's good fortune that in 1930 a couple of American short-story writers had hatched the magazine that would provide a stage for his hoboes. That year Martha Foley and Whit Burnett, husband and wife, founded *Story* magazine in Vienna, where they were working as foreign correspondents. *Story* aimed at doing for short fiction what Harriet Monroe's *Poetry* was doing for verse.

Martha Foley had originally conceived the magazine idea in 1925 while working on the *Los Angeles News*. A fellow journalist, Doug Tourney, was bemoaning that his old fiction market, *Smart Set*, was sunk, and its former editors, H. L. Mencken and George Jean Nathan, were using little fiction in their new *American Mercury*. "Let's you and I start a serious fiction magazine," Foley said. They talked it over, but Tourney felt that most of his energy would have to go into his newspaper column.

Five years later in Europe, when Eugene Jolas told Foley that he planned to quit running short fiction in *transition* magazine, she and Burnett decided to produce a mimeographed little magazine that would showcase first-rate stories. Then they discovered how cheaply it could be typeset and printed in a Vienna commercial shop, and *Story* began publishing. When Consolidated Press, the service for which the couple worked, was dissolved, they moved to Majorca. Their magazine's reputation continued to grow. Edward O'Brien printed eight pieces from *Story* in *The Best American Short Stories*. Random House offered to take the magazine under its wing, but Martha and Whit were down to their last fifty dollars and couldn't afford boat fare back to New York. By a stroke of luck, Martha got a small inheritance just then, which allowed them to return and accept. *Story* then entered its heyday, and during these peak years, 1934–36, it had a circulation of twenty-thousand or more. It published for the first time in America serious fiction by Peter De Vries, William Saroyan, Robert Traver, Jesse Stuart, George Milburn, Jerome Weidman, Emily Hahn, John Cheever, Ludwig Bemelmans, Carson McCullers —and Edward Anderson. Thus, *Story* offered the serious short-story writer one of the largest American audiences ever during those three years of the middle thirties. Fate arranged that Edward Anderson, unable to get the hang of the pulp formula, should produce his superb hobo stories during the magazine's peak years. *Story* accepted two of them.

Random House looked upon *Story* as a discoverer of talent. Other publishers read it with great interest also, and *Story* joined with Doubleday Doran to offer a one-thousand-dollar prize and publication for a first novel. Doubleday Doran put up the prize money; the entrance requirement was that *Story* must have previously accepted a piece of fiction from the author. The judges were Martha Foley herself; Lewis Gannett, book critic of the *New York Herald Tribune*; and Harry E. Maule, managing editor of Doubleday Doran.

The contest was a one-shot affair. *Story* had opened its three-year window to Anderson just as he began sending out serious short stories. Now he found himself eligible to send in his first novel to their contest.

The three judges of the novel contest all had considerable experience in objectively judging pieces of literature. Still, it is interesting to speculate on their backgrounds and opinions, which might have had some influence on their decision.

The most conservative of the three would appear to be Harry Edward Maule: thirty-one years old, an Episcopalian, one wife, one daughter. A small-town boy from Fairmont, Nebraska, he had become a newspaper reporter in Denver in 1903 but was working on a New York newspaper within two years. (All three judges had newspaper backgrounds.) He wrote the *Boy's Book of New Inventions* in 1912 and joined Doubleday; in the forties he would join Random House. Over a long career Maule edited a number of anthologies, including a Sinclair Lewis reader.

More to the left would seem to be Lewis Stiles Gannett, age forty-three, whose father was a Unitarian minister and whose mother was a Quaker. He had started out to be a naturalist but shifted to philosophy before graduating from Harvard in 1913; he had added an M.A. in economics in 1915, after a year of study at the universities of Berlin and Freiburg. As a pacifist, he joined the American Friends' Service Committee in France during World War I. When peace returned, Gannett joined the staff of the *Nation*; he began his "Books and Things" column in the *New York Herald Tribune* in 1931. He wrote two travel books, *Young China,* published in 1926, and *Sweet Land,* published in 1934. His first wife, Mary Ross, to whom he was married from 1917 to 1929, was an author. His second wife, Ruth Chrisman Arens, was an artist.

The third and perhaps most important judge was *Story* editor Martha Foley, thirty-seven years of age, whose Boston Irish background may have inclined her to sympathize with the underdog. She had spent some time in a Boston jail in 1920 for demonstrating in favor of voting rights for women. She was a friend of Eugene V. Debs, Tom Mooney, and liberal causes.

John Graves, essayist and short-story writer, knew Foley in the late forties at Columbia University as a "quite petite" woman "with dainty hands and feet of which she was obviously proud—she wore tiny expensive shoes, with very high heels on which she tottered rather than walked." Graves felt that "she had never been a very pretty woman, though probably rather sexy in youth." Graves quickly learned that even to hint there might be two sides to a labor dispute would stir her; "tears would start forming behind those thick glasses and she would start to wave her arms and shout about policemen clubbing workers, and we would suddenly be back in the Boston of the Sacco-Vanzetti riots."

She taught Graves in a creative-writing class composed largely of World War II veterans. Like most of the students in the class, Graves was genuinely fond of Foley, and willing to accept her flaws with her strengths. He called her approach to writing and literature "almost totally intuitive and feminine." Yet granting that Foley had "some blind spots," Graves felt "her taste was just about infallible."

The characters of Maule, Gannett, and Foley were of course three important elements in determining who would win the novel contest. A fourth was the times, which, as always, determined the length of a woman's skirt, the width of a man's necktie, the shape of a literary work. The era was quite naturally obsessed with the Great Depression. Americans gave up their optimism slowly after the Crash, but by 1932 they welcomed a song like "Brother, Can You Spare a Dime?" In 1933 Jack Conroy's novel, *The Disinherited,* appeared in bookstores. Socialism, communism, and other radical remedies stirred new interest. Left-leaning critics called for "proletarian novels," although there was some disagreement as to what such a thing might be.

With all this in mind, no one should be surprised that the three judges weeded and snipped until they were left with two novels about poor folks caught in the Great Depression. The three judges—Maule, the conservative with his eye on both the trends and the balance sheet; Gannett, the liberal intellectual; Foley, the liberal and feminist — swayed back and forth over the merits of the two finalists.

One of the books was *Hungry Men*. Telling his story of a musician turned into a hobo by the Depression, Edward showed himself a master of the flat, understated, uniquely American style employed by Sherwood Anderson, Ernest Hemingway, Dashiell Hammett, and others. *Not for Heaven* by Dorothy McCleary was the other. Also set in the grim thirties, this novel concerned itself with a widow, her daughter and son, and her horse. As they weather the Depression, the widow becomes a memorable and believable character.

Edward's work was by then being handled by the literary agency of Brandt and Brandt, specifically by Bernice Baumgartern of that firm. In February of 1935, she sent the following telegram to him in New Orleans:

PRIVATE CONFIDENTIAL NOT TO BE RELEASED UNDER ANY CIRCUMSTANCE TO ANYONE STOP DOUBLE AWARD FOR CONTEST YOURS AND ONE OTHER EACH GETTING FULL PRIZE PROBABLY ANNOUNCED NEXT WEEK PUBLICATION AUGUST STOP ISN'T IT GRAND STOP SEND AIR MAIL PHOTOGRAPH AND FULLEST BIOGRAPHICAL MATERIAL STOP DONT TELL ANYONE

Although both prize-winning novels dealt with contemporary hard times, the situation of the author of the other book was worlds different from Edward Anderson. Dorothy McCleary was a New York housewife hard pressed for cash for her family. "This [prize money] comes as a godsend to us," she told an interviewer at the time. "I was fired as head of the bathroom department of a Brooklyn department store during the banking holiday, and we have had a perfectly beastly time ever since." Her husband, H. M. Hamilton, was a professional literary critic and the associate editor of a monthly magazine for writers called *The Editor*. They had one child, a son. Before marrying Hamilton, whom she had known since early childhood, Dorothy had been on the professional stage, where she first appeared in a vaudeville skit entitled "Romance of the Underworld" and later became a member of the Wadsworth Stock Company. Although *Not for Heaven* was her first published novel, she had been writing short stories for twenty-five years; she labeled her early work "shallow and inconsequential." Her first published work was a cookbook for beginners written shortly after she married. Squeezing in time for her novel had not been easy.

She had risen each morning at 4:30, had a cup of tea and a piece of buttered bread, written till 6:00, fixed breakfast for her husband and child, and then gone off to her job as a store clerk. After *Not for Heaven,* McCleary would go on to publish two more novels and a how-to book for would-be writers. Dorothy McCleary and Edward Anderson would never meet.

With a regular salary coming in from the New Orleans newspaper, Edward had decided that a French Quarter hotel was no place for an expectant mother, so they moved into an apartment at 5912 St. Charles Avenue, an apartment in an older home that had been cut up into suites. The place was close to Tulane University and much quieter, but where Edward had walked to work from the hotel, he now had to rely on streetcar and bus to get around.

Anne suffered a miserable case of morning sickness. To distract her, Edward bought her an Atwater Kent radio, a table model. She could hear Fred Allen, Fanny Brice, Jack Benny, and Jack Pearl, as Baron Munchausen—all good company for anybody who liked to laugh. Anne's favorite still was "Amos 'n' Andy." She could also tune in the New York Philharmonic, although most hours of the day she would be more likely to find the Phil Spitalny Orchestra, Guy Lombardo, or the like playing the current hit songs: "The Music Goes Round and Round," "Red Sails in the Sunset," "I Can't Get Started with You," or Irving Berlin's wonderful "Dancing Cheek to Cheek." Anne liked opera, and she fell in love with "Summertime," "Bess, You Is My Woman," and "I Got Plenty of Nothin'" from George Gershwin's new *Porgy and Bess.*

Mardi Gras was an explosion of happiness. Edward took Anne to the parade, world famous for its splendor and variety. In Chicago gangsters might machine-gun one another, but in New Orleans few muggers lurked around the corner. Edward and Anne felt safe in the streets jammed with celebrants. Edward gave pennies to street urchins who would then improvise lively jigs and tap dances for Anne's amusement.

In contrast, much of the news that Edward saw come across the desk of the newspaper where he worked in 1935 was bad. Herr Hitler conducted his Blood Purge in Germany that year. The *Morro Castle* burned in the Atlantic off New Jersey and 137 passengers lost their lives. Even good news could be grim, as in the case of G-men shooting John Dillinger outside a Chicago theater. The New Dealers had put a tourniquet on the Depression, but millions were still out of work, and many older Americans boosted the plan of an elderly physician, Dr. Francis Townsend, to produce national prosperity by giving old folks a guaranteed income.

The St. Charles apartment was small, perhaps large enough for a "little love nest" celebrated by so many songwriters of that day, but too small for "baby makes three," and certainly too small if visitors came. So Edward and Anne moved again, this time to a small house on the shores of Lake Pontchartrain. Soon after, Dorothy Anderson, Edward's youngest sister, came for a visit; Anne and Dorothy continued to get on well.

In America books are traditionally published in the spring and fall. Doubleday decided to move up *Hungry Men* from fall to spring, from August to May. The book had also been named, along with Dorothy McCleary's *Not for Heaven,* as a Literary Guild selection, and both the contest winners were published under one cover for the Guild membership. Anderson found himself an author between hard covers.

The publication schedule for babies is somewhat less firm. Edward and Anne were expecting their first child in July or August, but she arrived on May 30, almost too early. They almost lost her, but the physicians at Touro Infirmary saved the little girl. They named her Helen Ann. The Helen was for her grandmother Anderson, the Ann for her mother. Thus, Edward Anderson found himself the author of a published book and the father of a daughter that May, in both cases somewhat earlier than he expected.

In June, Pearl Bates came to help her daughter with the new grandchild. Also in June, Anderson received word from Edward O'Brien that his story, "Bare Legs," had been named to the Honor Roll of O'Brien's famous annual volume, *Best American Short Stories.* O'Brien, who would die at the age of fifty-one in London during the blitz, had begun the series in 1914. Reading roughly eight thousand stories a year while he looked through practically every magazine in America, O'Brien had built a justly deserved reputation for finding talent. Anderson could only be impressed when he received a note from Oxford dated June 20: "I shall be grateful if you will send me a short biographical note. . . ."

Hungry Men was wonderfully timely. In the first seven months of 1935 alone, 269 hoboes died trying to board Missouri Pacific trains. The most famous racial incident of the era was being argued in the trial of the Scottsboro Boys, a group of young black hoboes who were accused of raping two white women hoboes aboard a freight car. At the same time, critics were devoting very serious attention to the proletarian novel, a type of fiction concerning workers caught up in a struggle against the capitalist system. In New York and Paris that year, communist-encouraged Writers Congresses, attended by some of the most respected literary figures, discussed proletarian fiction.

This timeliness helped *Hungry Men* get serious attention in the most influential publications. Mark Van Doren in the *Nation* was cool because he felt Anderson's hero "does not succeed in seeming representative," and B. R. Redman in the *Saturday Review of Literature* felt Anderson "had been studying in the wrong laboratory" and failed "for purposes of prophecy"—both of which were Marxist objections. On the other hand, Otis Ferguson in the *New Republic* liked this "well done, if episodic book" and commended its "firm quiet realism." Horace Gregory in *Books* said Anderson had chosen a timely subject and treated it in prose that is "crisp and firm."

In Great Britain the book was also treated seriously. "Both [the hero] and the other more transitory characters are described with convincing knowledge," admitted the *Times Literary Supplement*, "but . . . this kind of thing has been done before and done more distinctly." Elizabeth Bowen in the *New Statesman* liked it, found it "excellently written," and felt the book should be read "because of its matter-of-factness and gusto." *John O'London's* believed "the style, the extreme nakedness of presentation, the slang 'like an animal talking,' owes everything to Mr. Ernest Hemingway," but in sum it said that Anderson "has given us a tale seen with his own eyes." The *Time and Tide* reviewer thought Anderson had caught "the peculiarly modern horror" that he identified as "the weakening of the spirit in adversity because of the sickening contrast between the contemporary social reality and the almost universally current Utopian dreams." On both sides of the Atlantic, few reviewers of any hue would have disagreed with the *Edinburgh Evening News* opinion that "realism abounds in Mr. Anderson's vividly written narrative."

Although Anderson had sporadic connections with Abilene in the twenties and thirties he was still a shadowy figure to many persons in the little West Texas city. Then suddenly, in 1935, Abilene learned that somebody named Anderson who had been associated with the *Morning News* had written a prize-winning novel.

The publisher of the newspaper was George Anderson. The sports editor was Prexy Anderson. In his column, "Prexy's Muse," the sports editor related:

> My face becomes especially red recalling a kind old lady to whom I was introduced several weeks ago. The exclamations of flattery she manufactured indicated well she would not have been any more impressed had she just met Roosevelt, King George, Emily Post and Jerry the Greek in a body.
>
> It did strike me as strange that a person who wouldn't know a forehand smash from a double reverse around left end should get so worked up over an athletic scribe, but momentarily I was making the most of the situation.
>
> Then the great light suddenly dawned.
>
> "You," I suggested, "must have made an error. I am not the author of the novel."
>
> The resulting letdown "Oh-uh" sounded a great deal like the latest slump of the St. Louis Cardinals, and the kind old lady hurried away in ill-concealed disappointment.

8. A Bandit behind the Walls

Edward Anderson came home one day to the little house on the shore of Lake Pontchartrain and announced, "I think I'll write another novel."

He would have a hard time if he tried to write a book inside the crowded lakeshore house. Standing out in his yard he didn't feel crowded; he could look out over Pontchartrain lapping across 625 acres north of New Orleans. Inside the little house, on the other hand, Edward rubbed against four other souls: his wife, new daughter, sister, and mother-in-law. That was a great many for a fellow who liked to have one friend at a time.

Pearl Bates had been a teacher before she married a policeman, and a schoolteacher could only be fascinated by the history found in every New Orleans street. She was also a painter, and painters tend to fall in love with the architectural charm of the old city. Pearl, however, had to spend much of her time helping Anne with little Helen, even though little Helen had become a model baby after the crisis of her birth. Pearl was an expert, having tackled the job of raising her twins, L. E., Jr., and Ruby Norene (called "Son" and "Sis" in the Bates family).

Dorothy Anderson was at a loss in helping with an infant. She was a skilled secretary—she had in fact typed a final draft of *Hungry Men* for Edward—and being a secretary would remain her vocation; she would never marry.

As a young mother Anne was plenty busy, but, young and ever the optimist, she took the new novel-writing project without blinking.

Edward bought a car. With the family bank account swollen by the thousand-dollar Doubleday-*Story* prize, he paid eight hundred dollars cash. He and Anne chose a Ford, gray, one of the new V8s like the ones bank robber Clyde Barrow chose for their pep as well as the solid body structure capable of deflecting most small-caliber bullets.

When Edward gave two weeks' notice to his newspaper, the three women began packing. A single man travels light; a married couple with a baby and two additional women relatives travels with considerably more luggage. That gray Ford was well filled when it headed out for Abilene late in 1935.

Edward had in mind a novel about bandits. Two decades of violent crime plagued the nation following World War I. Newspapers loved it. Anderson himself had covered the trial of the Santa Claus bank robber, Marshall Ratliff, who had disguised himself in red suit and cotton whiskers to head a gang in the holdup of the First National Bank of Cisco, Texas, in December of 1927. In the early thirties, perhaps egged on by the Depression, young men everywhere began careers as stickup men. Dillinger, Bonnie and Clyde, Harvey Bailey, Raymond Hamilton, Pretty Boy Floyd, and Baby Face Nelson were only the better-known names among the horde of mad-dog bandits.

Anderson knew a lot about crime from prying out facts for his newspaper and true detective magazine writing. But like his contemporaries, Fitzgerald and Hemingway, he needed an almost autobiographical closeness to events in order to write believable, publishable fiction. He planned to supply this by interviewing a real bandit. Nobody much outside the family knew it, but a cousin of his was serving a life sentence in Huntsville for armed robbery. He told Texas authorities his name was Roy Johnson. Under another name he was wanted in Oklahoma, where he had escaped the prison to which he was sentenced for still other robberies. He feared identification by his real name, because murder charges awaited him if he were extradited to Oklahoma. Roy had visited in the Anderson household back when E. H. and Ellen were rearing their children at Ardmore, back before he strayed from the straight and narrow. He impressed Imogene, a little girl then, as "a very fine, handsome man." As the oldest, Edward would have known Roy best.

When the gray Ford finally came into Abilene—Edward made Anne drive much of the way—at the end of the long road from New Orleans, the young couple dropped Dorothy at her parents' home and went to stay with Pearl and "Son" Bates.

To get to talk to Roy, Anderson worked through his former em-

ployer William McCraw, now attorney general of Texas. From Mc-
Craw, the novelist got a letter of introduction to the authorities at the
prison in Huntsville, where the man in charge was Lee Simmons, the
tough old ex-sheriff who had hired Frank Hamer to run Bonnie and
Clyde to earth.

When Edward and Anne drove into Huntsville in 1935, the grim
towers of the Texas State Penitentiary seemed to glower down on the
town's five thousand law-abiding residents. Commonly called "The
Walls," the prison rose on Twelfth Street, just three blocks east of the
courthouse. This little town in the eastern part of the state was important historically as the home of General Sam Houston, liberator and
first president of the Texas republic; it also contained his imposing
grave marker, a ten-thousand-dollar monument by renowned sculptor
Pompeo Coppini. But it was the Walls that would dominate the imagi-
nations of Edward and Anne. The prison was old: Confederates had
filled it with Yankees captured during the Civil War. It now contained
various industries for its many inmate-workers: a shoe factory, a printing plant, a machine shop, a mattress factory, a candy factory, an
automobile license plate plant. The Walls also had its death row and
its electric chair, "Old Sparky," on which capital offenders took a ride
into the next world.

The Andersons had not brought little Helen Anne with them. From
Abilene they had driven first to Kerrville, where they had rented a
cottage. Pearl Bates had come to take care of the baby while Edward
and Anne traipsed off to the penitentiary to learn about criminal ways
for the new novel.

After the Andersons found a place to stay in Huntsville, Edward
got in touch with prison officials. Before he went to the Walls that
first day, Edward made sure he had writing paper and a couple of
well-sharpened pencils. Anne, a little scared, went with him. The prison
officials were courteous and correct. Edward and Anne met Roy in
a drab little brown room, glassed all the way around so that guards
could look in. The ceiling, the floor, and the rest of the walls were
wooden. No bars separated Roy from his visitors.

Roy was a large man physically; he towered over Edward. Although
he had once impressed little Imogene Anderson as being handsome,
prison cooking and middle age had made Roy flabby, giving him an
extra chin and a paunch. He was a dark man, dressed neatly in khaki

trousers and a khaki shirt open at the throat. No stripes; Anne had half expected stripes.

Roy spoke softly in a low voice, so low in fact that Edward now and then had trouble hearing him. Edward asked questions and wrote quickly, condensing the answers with the sure hand acquired in years of reporting. Anne listened, fascinated, wondering if Roy spoke so softly because he was afraid prison officials might be eavesdropping. Always full of questions, Anne also asked one on occasion. For more than two hours, Roy quietly described the outlaw life.

The Andersons returned the following day, and the next. Sessions in the little fishbowl of a room lasted up to three hours. Roy discussed avoiding lawmen by various ruses, keeping to country roads at night, hiding long hours in wretched little rooms lent by relatives or bootleggers or other sympathizers. He told of scouting possible robbery targets, of experiencing the surge of excitement pumped through his veins during a stickup, of fleeing amid police gunfire. Edward scribbled notes about the switching of license plates, about the stratagem of using one car in town and keeping a second car hidden in the country to carry the gang during holdups. He learned that the shrewd thief always had deliverymen hold newspapers and milk while he was away for a heist so as not to draw attention to his hideout. The sessions continued for a week.

When Anne finally steered the gray Ford back west toward Kerrville, Edward had thoroughly explored the mind of those fast-driving fugitives of the newspaper headlines, learned to see them as flesh-and-blood individuals who were hungry at mealtimes, sleepy at night, often frightened, capable of genuine romantic love for women and loyal friendships with fellow gangsters. When they drove out of Huntsville, however, Roy Johnson disappeared forever from their lives. Now and then, in future days, Anne would urge Edward to send Roy cigarettes at Christmas, a book, some money. Edward wasn't interested. A contact might somehow reveal Roy's true identity as a fugitive killer and doom him to ride Old Sparky. And of course Edward was never one to keep up personal contacts when he moved on. When the bandit novel was published, however, Edward dedicated it "TO MY COUSIN and MY WIFE, because there I was with an empty gun and you, Roy, supplied the ammunition and you, Anne, directed my aim."

Kerrville, more than a thousand feet higher above sea level than

Huntsville, sat in the Texas Hill Country, rugged and wooded. The Guadalupe River snaked past Kerrville on its way from Hunt to Center Point, Comfort, and even smaller settlements. Cattlemen and sheep herders managed to fatten small herds of their beasts in the low, wild hills, but plowboys who tilled the soil had a hard, lean time of it, raising mostly feed for livestock and just enough tobacco to smoke themselves.

Settlers had decided early on that if the place wasn't good for much else it was at least healthy. They promoted the Hill Country air as a cure for tuberculosis, and in the early years of the century whole camps of consumptives absorbed the clear Texas sunlight and drank the Guadalupe water, which, the chamber of commerce asserted, was "filtered clear to drinking purity by hundreds of feet of porous limestone" in the Edwards Plateau "formed during the Cretaceous era of the dinosaurs."

Tourists came too, and now that the area was more accessible because of the automobile, Kerr County entrepreneurs built tourist camps, those little lines of hotel rooms set separately along the fringes of an outdoor court, with parking space between them. Ranchers discovered they could charge visitors for hunting and fishing on their land; the going rates in the thirties ranged from two to five dollars a day. In general, Kerrville had awakened to a truth that a Texas governor would frame in words a quarter century later: "It's easier to pick a tourist than to pick a bale of cotton." But nobody became rich on visitors in 1935. The total population of Kerrville remained about forty-five hundred.

There were plenty of cabins in the hills that a visitor could rent cheaply. Edward had already found them a place, near an old TB hospital, three miles out of town. It was to this place that they returned from Huntsville, turning off the graveled highway, going through an arched gate and climbing a narrow, high-centered road through the cedars and frost-brown oaks. Edward would later make this rented house the hideout of the bandit-lovers in his novel:

> The wooden floors creaked under their feet. In this front room there was a blackened, empty stone fireplace and an iron army cot covered with a yellowed counterpane. There were two hide-bottomed rocking-chairs and a rickety breakfast table. In the windowed sleeping-room there was a broad iron bed, a huge dresser with a smoky mirror and two straight dining-room chairs. The kitchen had a three-burner grease-caked oil stove,

a sink, and an enamel-topped table. The bath had a shower and the toilet seat was split and part of it lay on the cement floor.

It was cheap, but the fear of tuberculosis hung unspoken in the back of Anne's mind there. She knew the place had formerly been rented to consumptives. She had a baby to look out for and a husband to take care of. Like the gun moll in the novel Edward wrote in that cabin, Anne went to work with lye soap, mop, and whitewash.

Pearl Bates had gone back to Abilene. As autumn dwindled into winter, Edward and Anne and little Helen Ann settled into their small house, now scoured clean. Anne struggled with the kitchen stove, a cranky old monster. Edward, fortunately, wasn't bothered by the change to plain fare from the more elaborate victuals that in New Orleans were as close as the corner grocery or the restaurant down the street. For Anne, however, the stove meant a battle three times a day, and once "it nearly burned the house down." On another occasion, when Edward was gone, the stove smoked up the house so bad that mother and daughter had to sleep outside.

For writing Edward found the house ideal. To write he needed only a little privacy and a flat surface on which to spread his paper and notes. Like any experienced reporter who has banged out miles of copy in noisy newsrooms, he could even dispense with the privacy. But privacy helped. The nights at Kerrville seemed wrapped in primordial silence after the ever-present hum of New Orleans.

Every day Edward marched down the five steps leading off the little corner porch of the house, along the flagstone walk, and out along the open road for a brisk walk, a hike much longer than Anne would care for most days, a hike of several miles. He met some neighbors that way.

Hungry Men was the second book by a Texan to become a selection of the Literary Guild. Down the road just two miles from the Anderson cottage at Kerrville was another little house, occupied by J. Frank Dobie, author of *Coronado's Children,* the first Literary Guild selection by a Texan.

Dobie was forty-seven years of age at the time, a stocky man with a face as plain and honest as an Irish potato. Since he had grown up on a ranch near Beeville, his legs were bowed from years on horseback. He earned his keep by teaching English at the University of Texas in Austin, but he had already published four books and was

Anne, Helen, and Edward at Dunbar Court, their rented cottage near Kerrville

eager to write more. His first book, published in 1929, was *A Vaquero of the Brush Country,* which told the life of an old-time cowboy named John Young. Then, after *Coronado's Children* brought him fame, Dobie had published a book principally for young readers, *On the Open Range,* in 1931, which he followed in 1935 with *Tongues of the Monte.*

Dobie was a World War I veteran, and had in fact undergone surgery to make himself fit to volunteer for the U.S. Army in 1917. After being commissioned a lieutenant in the artillery, he had arrived in France just before the Armistice. Of much more long-term importance for Dobie's career, however, was the accident of his being assigned in 1914 to share a faculty office with folklorist Stith Thompson, who hit him up for a one-dollar membership in the Texas Folklore Society—the money to be used for that infant organization's first publication. Dobie later said that he had never heard of either the society or folklore up until that time. Thompson would go on to become one of the world's great names in folklore. Dobie also would rise to fame as a writer of southwestern folklore, although he always noted that he wasn't a folklorist in the strict scientific sense.

When he became friends with the Andersons, Dobie had a 1934–35 grant from the Rockefeller Foundation "to pursue folklore wherever I want to pursue it." Back in March of 1935, at about the time Dorothy arrived in New Orleans to visit the Andersons, poet Carl Sandburg was visiting Austin to lecture at the University of Texas. He met and liked Dobie. In a letter after the visit, Sandburg scribbled a description of Dobie's personality that his wife Bertha Dobie particularly liked: "You are the salt of the earth I was going to say but while thinking of you as made of the same plain red clay as the general run of Texas I had a flash that the hand of the Potter felt experimental and threw in honey kindling phosphorous, H_2SO_4 ashes sheepguts horseneck ironore coal radium songs beans jumping beans much else saying: we will see what this piece of humus can stand and not go under."

The place where Dobie lived at Kerrville was a summer house built by his mother, Ella Byler Dobie, during 1931 in the Methodist Encampment. The Dobies were all Methodists (Ella Dobie had fired her first mason there because he showed up to work on her house pie-eyed drunk). The flat-roofed cottage, its native stone walls unfaced inside, hugged the western slope of Mount Wesley, which, despite its name, is as gentle and unobtrusive a little hill as any in Texas. Anne never went inside this bachelor's den; Bertha Dobie had remained in Austin. When Edward wandered over for a visit on winter evenings, the two men could sit, a friendly glass of whiskey in hand, and talk while they toasted their shins in front of the fireplace.

Dunbar Court, where the Andersons roosted, was an easy drive from the Dobie cottage. There wasn't much traffic, perhaps fortunately, because Dobie was a terrible driver. The folklorist's sister Martha recalled that Dobie's wife "admired everything about him, and she said, 'Oh, Frank is such a wonderful driver,' but the wonder was he didn't kill himself in a wreck." She reminisced about a time when he was in Kerrville "and took the wheel of my own personal car. We were just batting around, just driving around, and we came to one of those gates you just hit—'bumper gates' I believe they're called—and he hit that gate like I don't know what! The thing swung around and crushed my license plate. He and my sister got out to look, and they began laughing hard, and so I thought I had better get out to see what the joke was. I didn't think it was so funny."

Dobie and Anderson had a few things in common besides their interest in writing. Like Anderson, Dobie was 5'8" tall, had worked on newspapers briefly—the *San Antonio Express* and the *Galveston News*—and had even thought of making a career of it, and he wanted to write fiction, although his tentative move toward it with *Tongues of the Monte* had not achieved critical or financial success.

Dobie, however, was seventeen years senior to Anderson's thirty years. And while he disparaged pedants all his life, Dobie had earned a B.A. at Southwestern University in Georgetown, Texas, and an M.A. at Columbia University before World War I. As for Anderson, the visit with John Knox to the McMurry College campus may well have been the only hour he ever spent in a college classroom, and in later life Anderson would gibe at college learning.

Anderson, always an enthusiastic walker, could stroll a mile or two across the hills and pastures. In the spring, the hills and pastureland would briefly intoxicate the eye with the blues and reds, yellows and whites of wild flowers — Indian blankets, bluebonnets, cornflowers — but in gray winter there was little hint of this colorful extravagance lying just beneath the skin of the cold terrain. He saw only the yellowed native grasses that had managed to thrust up through the hard caliche slopes around the hills, grasses, and the wintry live oak, shinnery oak, the mesquite and cedar trees. Even in winter there was an austere beauty.

Every day Anderson worked at bringing order and development to his mass of Huntsville notes. Johnson's actual story began with his first arrest and conviction, continued with his escape from prison with a handful of other convicts, went on through their crime rampage, stickups and hiding, romances with poor girls in search of any escape from their wretched, Depression-haunted lives. Then, his fellow desperadoes dead, Johnson had again been arrested, tried, and put in another penitentiary. Anderson had never been much good with plots. As many critics had noticed, *Hungry Men* threaded a loose sequence of events along a situation rather than a genuine plot. If Anderson could have manufactured plots, he would have been supporting himself with pulp stories the way John Knox did.

Anderson eventually decided to skip his hero's early life and begin with the prison break. Perhaps he had his own happy times with Anne in mind when he gave his protagonist a deep and romantic love affair in the heart of the novel. Finally, since it is a long-acknowledged truth that nothing rounds out a novel like death, he would end with a Bonnie-and-Clyde–like finale. For a motif, Anderson turned back to a note sounded many times, and twice explicitly, in *Hungry Men*. In one place, Acel Stecker tells Boats: "'I've thought that the difference between a bank president and a bank bandit is that the robbery of the banker is legal. The bandit has more guts." And this, Acel thinks, is the reason bandits become newspaper heroes. Much later, Acel tells Big Boy that he has seen a newspaper story about a bum getting five years for stealing eighty-five cents from a pay phone, and next to it the picture of a banker who got only a year in the pen when his bank failed. This was the theme that the holdup men in his second book would sound over and over: that bankers were just "thieves like us."

Anne and Edward got on well together in the solitude. He worked at his notes or his typewriter, he took his long walks, and Anne took care of Helen and the house. During his years as a journalist, Edward hacked out news stories all day and then went home at night to read a good book; but during those times he was working on a fiction project, he would not read the work of other writers. In the little cottage at Kerrville, it was Anne who read. Before her marriage she had read popular fiction and such nineteenth-century greats as Victor Hugo. Edward introduced her to Hamsun and Hemingway, taught her to savor the modern temperament in the pages of *Story* and in Arnold Gingrich's new magazine called *Esquire*.

Anderson had trouble with his friendships. He wrote well, and his preference for proletarian subjects touched the proper critical nerve in the "red thirties," but his inability to cultivate a network of lasting friendships undoubtedly hurt his career. Skill with words and story are the main gifts needed for a good literary novel; skill with people is needed to make a good literary career. Every human endeavor, even a supremely private one such as writing, has political aspects. Aside from his acquaintance with Stanley Walker, the closest Anderson came to forming a link with the better-known Texas writers was his friendship that winter in Kerrville with J. Frank Dobie. On a typical afternoon Dobie knocked at the door of the Anderson cottage. Edward was sitting with his notes spread out over the surface of the dining table, trying to make a plot out of scattered events, trying to give literary form to the broken, chaotic stuff that is life. Anne was changing little Helen's diaper, but she hastily clasped the safety pin and rushed to answer Dobie's knock.

Well, hello. Come in, come in.

Am I interrupting?

Not at all. Anne suffered a little from cabin fever.

Edward rose from his work and came in, smiling but watchful. Earlier John Knox had noticed that, although Edward was talkative enough and friendly enough, something inside Edward seemed to be held back, remaining watchful.

Dobie just wanted to talk a little. He had reached that point where a writer can no longer sustain the necessary daydream, the disciplined interior monologue that his words on paper reflect. When Dobie could no longer write, he often took a break by driving (what old cowboy would walk when he could ride?) over to the Andersons. Anne delighted him with her youth and optimism. She wanted to know everything under the sun: Did Dobie himself believe in Spanish treasure? Was college teaching more fun than newspapering? Didn't Bertha Dobie miss him back in Austin? Edward too enjoyed the visits, and was flattered by the attention of the older writer.

Dobie had a book with him. Dobie read all the time, was a true book addict who had to have a few pages of prose or poetry at intervals every day. He had been interested to learn that Edward did not read at all while he was trying to write.

This day Dobie asked again if that were so.

Yep, couldn't read while he was writing.

Well then, Dobie said he would give this copy of his new *Tongues of the Monte* to Anne.

He sat down, took out his pen, and wrote words to that effect inside the cover on the flyleaf of the book as an explanation of why he was dedicating it to Anne. As an afterthought, he added that he knew she would ask him questions about it, too.

Anne was flattered, and a little flustered. Edward, watchful and noncommittal, smiled. He would become increasingly irked with these visits in coming days, visits that came at Dobie's convenience and frequently upset Anderson's schedule.

For Dobie, the friendship was mixed with troubling elements also. Fate, kind to the author of *Hungry Men* in several ways, had not dealt Anderson a good moment to know the author of *Coronado's Children*. Dobie, the future Dr. Johnson of Texas letters, was still feeling his way. In 1935 Dobie had suffered a hard knock when he attempted to edge toward the novel genre by mixing fiction with folklore in *Tongues of the Monte*. When Dobie came to Kerrville that winter to escape his allergies, he was thinking over his failure, and he would eventually return to his tales of lost treasure in *Aztec Gold and Yaqui Silver*. But Dobie wanted very much to write fiction. Here at Kerrville he had stumbled upon a young man who had succeeded with seeming ease in his first novel, a young man whose reading might be wide and deep compared with that of most newspapermen, but it was shallow compared with Dobie's. The earlier Dr. Johnson was jealous of the seemingly easy theatrical success of his former pupil David Garrick, and Dobie would not be immune to such feelings.

On the surface friendly and outgoing, Dobie was a complex man who had a strong streak of cantankerousness. It was a streak that would come to the surface publicly the following April, when he would refuse to pay an Austin traffic ticket totaling two dollars, insisting instead on laying it out in jail.

The sensitive Edward thought he detected something patronizing in Dobie's behavior toward him, thought Dobie was "laughing when nothing funny had been said." Anne was quick to pick up on her husband's attitude and, with the loyalty of love, to adopt it. She decided she wasn't pleased with Dobie's comment in the book autograph about her asking questions.

Sometimes Dobie came clomping over in his boots at two in the morning, after a tiring writing session.

Hello, anybody still awake?

Ever Pollyanna, Anne came smiling in her housecoat to the door. But the noise woke the baby; Frank and Bertha Dobie to their sorrow had no children, and without first-hand experience it was hard for him to appreciate Anne's problem.

If Anderson had remained friendly with Dobie, he could probably have become involved with other authors, such as those who eventually made up the Texas Institute of Letters, and they could have provided an "old-boy network" to help out when his fortunes dipped. Friends can provide counsel, tip an author off that a publisher will pay for a bit of hackwork on, for example, a restaurant guide, mention an editing job that's open, gossip about current literary trends. It was not to be.

As his friendship with Dobie cooled, Anderson began thinking about his old pal, John H. Knox. He missed Knox in planning his second book. Anderson may have possessed a touch of genius, but he didn't know a tenth as much about fiction technique as the intellectual Knox, who was merely talented.

John and Mabel Knox had moved to the area north of Denver in Colorado. A freelancer supporting himself by writing can live where he chooses, and John chose Colorado because of its breathtaking beauty and because mountainous country was generally thought to be health-giving for consumptives such as Mabel.

Anderson had earlier obtained John's address from his family. From Kerrville, Anderson wrote one of his rare personal letters to Knox in Boulder (John would later say that it was the only letter from Anderson he ever received), suggesting that John and Mabel come to Kerrville. The Kerrville area was also beautiful and healthy, and Anderson mentioned that he had become acquainted with his neighbor, J. Frank Dobie.

Knox himself was meditating about this time on the problems of writing a novel. Knox had heard Thomas Wolfe make his famous speech on novel-writing at the University of Colorado Writers' Conference on August 6, 1935. The thirty-five-year-old Wolfe, then enjoying his first great popular success with the best-selling *Of Time and the River*, had jumped at the $250 writers' conference pay principally because he wanted to see the American West. When he arrived, however, Wolfe had been a trifle overawed by the presentations of other famous writers. These included Robert Frost and Robert Penn Warren (names that would have intrigued the poet in Knox most, although he had for the most part given up verse in order to support himself with magazine fiction). *Story* editors Martha Foley and Whit Burnett were also on the program, being fiction writers as well, along with many other authors of the day.

Knox, no small man himself, was awed at the size of Wolfe when he stood up at the conference lectern that evening. Wolfe stood 6'6" tall and weighed 250 pounds. His body seemed too vast for his face, with its sharp, upturned nose and a lower lip that jutted. His hair seemed longer and more unruly than usual that evening, and his dark eyes, normally penetrating, betrayed his nervousness. Wolfe, who could rattle on confidently and even arrogantly among familiars, who that evening had one of the best-selling novels in the nation, was shattered in front of this group.

This mountain of a man seemed to Knox and others to shake so much that the stage itself shook. After stammering his beginning, Wolfe gave up on his prepared speech. He pushed aside his notes. In direct, down-home words, Wolfe told his own story, a very personal story of how he had begun by trying to write plays, and when he had failed at theater, how he had begun his first book during 1926 while in London. He described the way he had remembered his North Carolina boyhood, a boyhood of sunny Southern days and small-town life remembered acutely in crowded, foggy London that autumn. He told how he returned to New York to finish the book, *Look Homeward, Angel,* which found a publisher only after he again had gone abroad.

After fifty minutes Wolfe paused with an apology for his wordiness. The audience would not let him stop. Knox joined the others in shouting for Wolfe to continue. So the huge novelist went on to relate the challenge of his second book, after the autobiographical first novel written "with a certain naked intensity of spirit." Finally, in Paris, Wolfe had again found that the alien setting made him strongly visualize America, and he began writing a torrent of scenes, events, and conversations, all set down in longhand in ledgers, without a tight plan. The need to write possessed him, drove him. He moved on to England, where he wrote from October through March, and there he began to give some shape to his work. He told how he finally returned to America with 300,000 or 400,000 words that could hardly be called a novel, how he settled in Brooklyn and continued to pour forth prose, unable to sleep at night, walking the streets and observing the horrors of the modern city. He related how editor Maxwell Perkins had finally joined him to cut, rewrite, and shape a manuscript of more than a million words into publishable form, his *Of Time and the River.*

Wolfe talked to the Boulder audience for an hour and forty minutes in all, striving to communicate the truth about the backbreaking work involved in his novels. After it was over, Knox said, "That was the best talk I ever heard in my life by a writer."

The crowd, wrung out with emotion, left the auditorium with similar feelings. Wolfe's talk eventually became the basis of *The Story of a Novel,* which was first serialized in the *Saturday Review of Literature* in December of 1935 and published as a book by Scribner's in April of 1936, just two years before Wolfe's death.

When Knox received Anderson's letter saying he was writing a bandit novel in Kerrville, Knox was intrigued because, for one thing, Anderson mentioned Dobie, and both John and his father admired Dobie's work. More important, John knew that his friend Eddie's first novel had, like Wolfe's, been strongly autobiographical. How was Anderson overcoming the proverbial problems in writing a second one?

9. Kerrville

More than seven hundred miles of road, very narrow road, a good part of it unpaved, lay between Boulder, Colorado, and Abilene, Texas. John Knox had to push on for long hours behind the wheel in this long first stride of the nine-hundred-mile journey to see Eddie. Mabel Knox became weary—it would show in her dark eyes—and their worry about her tuberculosis always hovered in the background.

The timing was right for a visit to his parents and sisters in Abilene; it was the Christmas season. Dr. Knox heard with interest John's description of the Thomas Wolfe speech in Boulder, of the huge novelist's shaky beginning, of John's belief in Wolfe's overwhelming sincerity. Dr. Knox was also interested to learn that J. Frank Dobie was in Kerrville. Mrs. Knox and the girls—Lucille, Ruth, and Anna—were more interested in how Mabel had made do for herself and John in cold, high Colorado during the waning days of autumn.

John now supported his household adequately, if not luxuriously, without having to pick up a shoe clerk's measuring stick again. He did it with "blood and terror." John regularly sat down and launched his two-fingered attack on his old typewriter to produce such stories as "By the Tale," published in *Clues Detective*; "Those Who Dwell in Coffins," in *Dime Mystery*; and "The Blood Moon," in *Horror Stories*. He had acquired a New York literary agent. Even though he wasn't writing poetry, he could not stop thinking of himself as a poet, and a newspaper feature on him in the *Dallas Journal* by Hilton Greer, a journalist who was also an established poet, talked of Knox as a promising young Texas bard.

As John and Mabel started for Kerrville, a fateful 1936 was in the offing. Alvin Karpis, "Old Creepy Eyes," one of the last mad-dog bandits, would be taken alive that year, and Bruno Hauptmann would be electrocuted for kidnaping the Lindbergh baby. The white German fighter Max Schmeling would defeat the black American Joe Louis on a technical knockout in the ring, but another black American, track star Jesse Owens, would triumph in the Berlin Olympics to embarrass the race-conscious Nazis. Hitler would invade the Rhineland, and the Spanish Civil War would begin. Americans everywhere would laugh at knock-knock jokes, and audiences in New York's Rainbow Room laughed loudly when a new entertainer named Edgar Bergen routed his jokes through a dummy he called Charlie McCarthy. *The Toast of New York* would be one of four pictures made by Edward Arnold in Hollywood. Edward G. Robinson would make *Bullets or Ballots* with Humphrey Bogart and Joan Blondell and would reluctantly autograph his photograph for the ambassador of his native Rumania, where his Jewish forebears had been mistreated. Edward VIII, smitten by American divorcee Wallis Warfield Simpson, would create "the love story of the century" by abdicating the English throne to marry her.

From Abilene, John steered his car toward Kerrville over the steep-shouldered roads. Highways generally went through the middle of Texas towns then, but there were only a few villages and some not-very-extensive county-seat towns built around courthouse squares — Coleman, Brady, the old German settlement of Fredericksburg — to slow him and Mabel. Even though Edward had sent instructions for getting to the Anderson place, John would have have some difficulty finding it. A Kerrville old-timer in bib overalls, seated downtown on a high curb, could point the way.

Edward and Anne were glad to see the road-weary travelers when they arrived. Edward may have needed only one friend at a time, but he needed that one. Anne had liked John since he had inconspicuously relieved her of that glass of booze back in Abilene in 1934. Anne and Mabel, however, had little to say to each other. Anne was interested in ideas and books, but Mabel, after more than two years with the intellectual John, had heard enough about theories and concepts to last her quite a while, thank you. Anne's main interest was really her baby; Mabel's two children were with her first husband, so talk of babies would not be comfortable for her. When she said anything at all, Mabel mostly complained that she couldn't remember to take the pills that her doctor had prescribed for her tuberculosis.

A notebook full of facts and freedom from regular employment were two elements that enabled Edward to write *Hungry Men.* John H. Knox had been the third important element—the intellectual stimulus and sounding board. When Knox arrived in Kerrville, Anderson once again had all three of those elements in place.

John wanted to meet Dobie, so Eddie introduced the two, but relations between Anderson and Dobie had cooled to the point that Knox never saw them together again. However, Knox liked Dobie, and Dobie liked Knox, who almost immediately decided that Dobie was "a great man as well as a great writer," and later said that he "never knew a really important person who could put you so at ease with his openness and plainness." Dobie was a man, John believed, who was "incapable of putting on side." Knox had even written a poem, "The Ballad of Francesca," based on one of Dobie's folk tales. The twenty-nine stanzas of the ballad had filled four pages of a 1929 issue of the *Southwest Review.* Dobie had liked the poem, and he said so to Knox.

In Dobie's or Knox's rented place, on wintry January evenings, the two of them would put their feet by the fire, pack their pipes with tobacco, light up, and talk. To feed their ravenous intellectual appetites, both men had looked into many a curious book. Dobie was of course also seventeen years older than thirty-year-old Knox, so their relationship had a professor-and-student quality with which both felt comfortable. Dobie found Knox quite different from the mildly cynical, always wary, and yet somehow naive Anderson. During one of these chats, Knox "very apologetically" showed Dobie one of his stories, "The Quiet Man," in a pulp magazine. Dobie read it carefully.

"Why, that would be a good story in anybody's magazine," said Dobie. The praise doubly warmed John because he thought Dobie would not "stoop to snow me."

They even talked about money. Knox had believed that *Coronado's Children* had made Dobie rich. The professor told him it just wasn't so, that he had made very little on the book and that he had lost out considerably on royalties when Southwest Press went broke and was sold to Doubleday. Knox was also surprised to learn that this professor did not want to return to the campus either. Dobie "dignified [Knox's] humble stuff" by saying that he wished he could make a living writing. Dobie said he was trying hard to sell more material to *Country Gentleman,* his best magazine market.

John, of course, disagreed with Dobie on some things. Dobie said

he didn't like Sam Houston, great-grandfather of John's friend Heitchew, and that he believed Houston's successes had been accidental,
that Houston had stolen the glory from Texas history's real hero, Ste-
phen F. Austin.

Unable at the time to dispute Dobie's opinion, Knox went off to
ponder the matter. He reasoned that "a lot of great men just weren't
born to be heroes," that "nobody can steal such a role." Knox decided
that "heroes just sprout up out of necessity" in certain eras. "Sam was
an archetype who arose at a time when they had to have him, and
just as uncoordinate Greece had to have big drunk Hercules, who was
far more important than Zeus and his bunch, Sam was the (almost
necessarily tainted) half-god link between little Greece and Heaven.
He gave them their identity." But as with so many good answers, John
thought it out after Dobie was gone from Kerrville.

Knox would later also question Dobie's judgment about some of
the sources behind one of his books. Knox knew one such man, a
Dobie source, in El Paso, who was "paling around" with former bandit Al Jennings and "Little Bob" Slaughter of the famous ranch family. Knox had even arranged to write of this man's adventures, but
Knox finally decided Dobie's man was "a phony and an awful liar"
and that some of his yarns would have been rejected by Baron Munchausen. Dobie had taken this source much more seriously.

The friendship between the older writer and the younger remained
healthy despite such small points of disagreement, small points John
kept mostly to himself. He liked Dobie's pragmatic good humor. One
day Knox was with a small group of young men who were discussing
among themselves the possibility of illegally shooting a wild turkey
to eat. The chief problem under discussion was how to get rid of the
feathers. Dobie, puffing his pipe, listened a few minutes. "You kill
the bird," he finally said. "I'll take care of the feathers."

Eventually Dobie would have to leave Kerrville because the bloom
of the foliage there tormented his hay fever. One day not long before
his departure, John walked over to Dobie's and found the folklorist
behind the cottage, squatting to split kindling.

Dobie said something gloomy about the possibility that he might
return to the university in Austin.

"I guess the students aren't much of an inspiration," said Knox.

"No, nor the faculty either," snorted Dobie.

Anderson finally got a manuscript for his bandit story together and shipped it to Bernice Baumgartern at Brandt and Brandt. But the violence in the novel had the effect of garlic dropped into a stew; it gave flavor to the whole out of proportion to its size. One element of the novel was bank robberies, but it was the only element Edward's agent could see. She suggested Edward sell his novel as a serial to *True Detective* or the like. Several editors of detective magazines knew his work, after all, and they valued it highly. The suggestion hit Edward wrong. A detective magazine? He had written *They're Thieves Like Us* as a serious novel, and he damned sure intended for it to go between hard covers, as a serious novel should.

Edward talked the matter over with John. Knox knew Anderson to be a "real craftsman with words" who took great pains to avoid clichés, great pains to keep his metaphors fresh and original. In 1934 the two friends had thoroughly chewed over a thousand various points of *Hungry Men,* beginning with the first scene and whether "anemic" was the right adjective to describe the flow of a drinking fountain. The upshot of their conversations was that Edward would run his manuscript through the typewriter again to remove anything that made it sound like a detective magazine serial. Although *Hungry Men* had hardly challenged the sales of *Green Light* by Lloyd C. Douglas or *Good-bye, Mr. Chips* by James Hilton during the year it was published, the critics on both sides of the Atlantic had discussed it seriously, and Anderson felt that he had to write a worthy successor.

After supper one night John and Mabel came to visit the Andersons. John and Eddie drank three fingers of now-legal bourbon. John got out his pipe. Eddie picked up his own pipe from the table; he had put aside his customary cigarettes and, like John, smoked a pipe that winter in Kerrville. Smoking a pipe seemed somehow conducive to deep thinking. They conducted the solemn ritual of opening the tobacco pouch and filling the pipe bowl with the brown weed, packing the mild narcotic with a finger, striking a wooden match to fire the leaf fragments. The ritual moved at the dignified pace of a symphonic largo, and it discouraged hasty logic, snap judgments. With the same meditative pace, John one day walked up into the hills and spent half a day, one of those warm days that God drops now and then into Texas Hill Country winters, using his pocketknife to patiently scrape all the paint off an empty coffee can, all except for the likeness of a ship painted on it. When he had finished, the shiny can with the ship on it became a humidor for his tobacco.

Anne noticed that the pipe-smoking John and Edward talked often about the "intelligentsia," a word from Soviet Russia frequently on the lips of writers in the thirties, but one with an exotic ring for a Methodist girl from Fort Worth. Edward and John obviously considered themselves members of the intelligentsia. Although they sent up clouds of pipe smoke, Anne abstained from smoking that winter because she again was pregnant, and she worried about the effect that nicotine might have on her baby.

Knox thought of that other pipe smoker, Dobie. John told Edward that he and Dobie had been discussing writing, that he had shown Dobie one of his short manuscripts, a piece about cowboys called "Coolies on Horseback," depicting cowboys not as heroic figures but as dunces working for starvation wages. Dobie had not liked it much, and Anderson of course didn't like Dobie's evaluation. Knox found the reasons Anderson gave for his dislike of the older writer "too esoteric to grasp." Eddie even talked about a "certain expression" on Dobie's face as one reason for his dislike.

John didn't argue, but he had already decided that Dobie was correct in his literary judgment, that the piece was a "stacked-card smart alec job." John had started thinking of his cousin, a lank cowboy who was a "generous, gentle big-brother image with a whole bunch of kids of his own who loved him till his dying day." He decided not to attack his cousin's craft; he would not submit the story to his agent.

The bourbon went around again. Anne had put little Helen down for the night in the next room, and she and Mabel joined their husbands. Mabel had on a dress with a plunging neckline, frilly and feminine, too feminine, in Anne's opinion, for the rustic life they were leading in Kerrville. Mabel's dramatic appearance, coupled with her bland talk, bored Anne. Anne concentrated her attention on the men, who were engaged in their ideological debates.

The topic changed from writing to religion, and the men debated as to whether they should be classified as atheists or agnostics. Edward sat up straight in his chair, unlike John, who slumped on his backbone. Edward gave the impression of never wanting to get caught off guard, like an old outlaw who would drink only with his back to the wall. As the evening wore on, Knox would find himself silently considering his friend's dislike of Dobie, his way of suddenly dropping friends. Mentally, Knox tried to formulate Anderson's character into words. Eddie was "a born changeling, something like a leprechaun, not different in appearance, but different in some undefinable way" that simple people of an earlier age would have diagnosed as an imbalance of the bodily humors. Knox again observed there was "behind Eddie's eyes something pragmatic, wary, watchful." John felt his naiveté was an element of strength in Anderson's realistic writing, as it was in the paintings of Henri Rousseau. John also knew that Eddie "was sometimes unconsciously tactless, too frank, too blunt, in a humorless way." John qualified this by adding that Eddie "wasn't devoid of humor and could tell and laugh about incidents in which he came off second best."

Most days in Kerrville Anne was happy, even though the cabin in the hills was no Garden of Eden. She was twenty years old now, had an eight-month-old baby to care for, and a cranky old oil stove to cook on. Kerrville might offer a retreat for Edward, but it was still the real world for Anne.

Edward was pleasant and affectionate, though. On the rare occasions when someone was available to sit with Helen, Anne accompanied Edward on his walks through the wooded hills. There in the tranquil woods he became the gallant and adventurous suitor again. They might stop to sit beneath a tree, kiss, become romantic. Anne loved walking with Edward. Still, if he was unhappy, especially those times when he was forced to work on the newspapers he despised in order to support his family, Edward, without ever raising his voice, would say things that barbed Anne painfully. Most of that would come later.

He went on little drinking binges at Kerrville, particularly when John showed up, but Anne supposed (correctly, for that era) that drinking was generally part of a writer's life. But Edward was all soberness and seriousness when he would sit down at the table to write. While he worked, Anne had some time to read, and Edward continued to steer his young wife to writers that he himself admired: Sherwood Anderson, Theodore Dreiser, Upton Sinclair, Emile Zola, Fyodor Dostoyevsky, James Farrell.

She also played a game in which she hunted difficult words in the dictionary and challenged Edward to define them. Anne never caught him; he always knew.

As the bandit novel took shape, Edward asked Anne questions. What would Keechie, the young woman, say while the bandit couple was in the car? If Bowie said this, what would Keechie . . . ? Anne felt herself inside the skin of the novel's heroine.

A dog was an exception to Edward's one-friend rule. The Andersons had a big German shepherd named Silver, who raised the hue and cry if any stranger strayed too near their relatively isolated house. They tried to keep Silver close by; neighboring sheep raisers hated all dogs. Knox also had canine companionship, shaggy, affectionate little mongrels who were generally at his heels. John inspired warm feelings among all fellow creatures — men, women, mutts. When John went to town, the dogs lay down by the gate and patiently awaited his return.

One gloomy afternoon, the two couples set out in the Andersons' gray Ford to buy some booze for the men. When they left, the February skies were cloudy and threatening. Then the rain began. Anne drove back after dark, barely able to find the way over the country road, while the wipers, like twin metronomes, swung back and forth steadily to clear the raindrops from the windshield. As they turned into the gate by the Knox place, the car's headlights revealed two limp, furry forms. John's dogs lay by the gate dead. Anne braked. John got out to examine them. Someone had shot them.

John wept. Anne, now out and examining the bodies herself, looked up to find this massive man, the most thoughtful and gentle of persons, crying, his tears mingled with the raindrops. Anne had never seen a grown man weep before, and the sight moved her profoundly. Since sheep men hated pet dogs, which often killed sheep, the four concluded that a sheep raiser had slain them.

The image of the little mongrels and John in tears lingered with Edward and Anne as they drove back to their house. The Knox dogs were so small they were probably harmless. Silver, large enough to kill a sheep, a horse, or even a man, barked with delighted anticipation when they pulled up at their door.

Gradually Anderson's novel, which he called *They're Thieves Like Us* (an editor cut the first word), came together. The book's title comes from the remark frequently on the lips of T. W. (T-Dub) Masefield, who, as the oldest and most experienced of Anderson's bandit trio, is something of a philosopher. According to T-Dub, the followers of many respectable professions — bankers, police officers, pharmacists, politicians — are "just thieves like us."

T-Dub Masefield is forty-four years old, and the bank holdup at Zelton is his thirtieth such robbery. T-Dub's wisdom falters, however, when he falls for and marries a tall country girl named Lula with a tattoo of a red heart on her hand.

Elmo Mobley, known to the newspapers as "Three-toed Mobley" and to his friends as "Chicamaw," is also an experienced stick-up man. He is thirty-five and like Anderson, part Indian. He drinks hard and often.

Bowie A. Bowers, the third bandit, is the central figure. Only twenty-seven years old. Bowie has only one bungled holdup behind him, but in that single crime he killed a man. While the three bandits are holed up at Keota, Oklahoma, following their escape from Alcatona prison, Bowie falls in love with Keechie Mobley, the daughter of Chicamaw's cousin, Dee Mobley, who hides them in a room behind his filling station–grocery store.

The characters are sketched in varying degrees of detail, and Bowie and Keechie receive the most attention. Their pasts are described, providing explanations for their present actions. Bowie throughout the novel worries about his mother, a woman married often and to husbands of varying quality. He mails her five hundred dollars, but worries that her current spouse will "get every damned bit of it."

Keechie tries to steer Bowie down a path that will keep him alive, first to the former tuberculosis colony at Antelope Center and then, after another robbery, to New Orleans. But when he insists upon dangerous enterprises, Keechie is faithful to him. Their honeymoon in hiding gives a bittersweet quality to the last half of the book.

Anderson's friend, John Knox, once said that *Thieves* "fairly reeks the hard dry ambience of Texas-Oklahoma, the smell of dust and hot mesquite gum, of crude oil and dried cowchips." Some places in the novel, such as Dallas and New Orleans, appear under their true names. Others are described in detail, but their names have been altered. "Keota" might be Ardmore, although the reader sees only a filling station–grocery store there, hardly enough evidence to judge by. Other spots have a distinct Texas twang. "Zelton," where the bandits hold up their second bank, is described as having a skyline with "the fourteen story hotel, the standpipe, the college buildings on the hill." All this sounds like Abilene in the thirties — the then-new Wooten Hotel and McMurry College on its hill. "Gusherton" is probably oil-boom Ranger, and "Clear Waters" probably Sweetwater, both towns within a fifty-mile radius of Abilene. "Antelope Center," with its camp for consumptives, has all the landmarks of Kerrville and the camp where Anne fought the oil stove and cared for little Helen while Edward wrote his novel.

Thieves Like Us isn't in the classic proletarian mold described by Malcolm Cowley. It doesn't concern a strike, and it doesn't center around a wise old radical who, before he is clubbed to death by strikebreakers, passes the torch to a young convert. It does, however, concern three young men of the working class who apparently have been drawn into crime by circumstances, chiefly poverty.

None of them is a Mack the Knife. Chicamaw is probably the closest to being an unregenerate scoundrel. Keechie, his second cousin, says, "That Chicamaw Mobley has never liked anything but trouble all his life." He stays drunk much of the time, and prefers prostitutes for companions. Chicamaw's plans for the future are hazy, perhaps another escape to Mexico where "fifty pesos will get you anything you want." More immediately, he wants to get money to his family so they will have money to bury him: "Bowie, they ain't going to catch me floating around in no tank in them doctor schools if they ever get me. That's what they do if you can't pay the undertaker. They'll throw you in one of them tanks and carve on you."

T-Dub, the philosopher, the wise old head of the group, has spent most of his forty-four years in crime also. In a fit of reminiscence, T-Dub recalls robbing the bank at Morehead when he was only a child. "Sawed me off a bar and crawled through and got fourteen dollars in pennies." He was a poor boy, "getting me some bicycle money. It was the day after Christmas." Unlike Chicamaw, T-Dub plans to leave crime after he has "about fifty thousand salted away," which he hopes to invest at a good return. Then he plans to find a crooked surgeon to remove his fingerprints, "and I'd grow me a beard about a foot long and rear back up in them Kentucky hills on a little farm and let the mistletoe hang on my coat tail for the rest of the world." Despite T-Dub's choice of banditry as a career, his values make him basically a petit bourgeois. He proves this by legally wedding Lula and signing his real name to the license.

Of the trio, Bowie is least a crook. Bowie has been roustabouting with a carnival since he was fourteen. He had gone along out of curiosity to watch some companions rob a safe. Discovered, the others had run for it, but Bowie had been trapped by a man with a gun.

He would prefer an honest life. "You'd see me following a one-eyed mule and a Georgia walking stock if I had to and what's more, like it. If I could." Early in their crime spree, Bowie says, "Five thousand, gentlemen, and I'm backing off." But after the Gusherton robbery, Bowie's share is more than six thousand dollars and he is unable to extricate himself and Keechie from the criminal life.

As Anderson worked hard to graft his own acute sensibility onto the grubby adventures of a minor crook, he knew that his money was running out. A work of art is seldom created under ideal conditions; it is created on earth by a harassed mortal who has mundane problems shouting for attention. Unlike Dobie, Anderson had no Rockefeller grant money, or any other such funds to prop him up. He knew that each day bled a little more out of his bank balance. Sometimes little Helen cried in the next room; sometimes even Anne got worked up over the oil stove and became quarrelsome. About the only thing Anne really liked about the rustic life in the hills was Edward's friend John, and Edward would wonder to his family if Anne didn't like John too much. Edward was capable of jealousy.

One afternoon, Edward walked over to the Knox place and found John, as usual, with a drink in his hand. John poured his colleague three fingers of bourbon, and they sat down to discuss writerly problems. John had applauded Edward's decision to reject the idea of detective magazine publication, and they put their heads together over many of the book's problems as Anderson hammered out his revision. That afternoon seemed no different from the others to Knox, with frank and open discussion of the book, professional objectivity expressed on both sides.

When John strolled over to the Anderson cottage the next day, however, he walked through the door into an atmosphere charged with hostility. Edward accused his friend of looking down his nose at Edward's work: Y'all fellows who went to college never get over it; you think you know everything. Just because you sell a couple of ghost stories to Frank Munsey's pulps. . . . John flared a little, but even then it seemed to him as silly as a schoolyard melodrama when one kid makes faces at another. Although the charges were vague, Knox learned in the heated exchange that Anderson believed that his friend disparaged his work in general and the crook novel in particular.

Edward gave his baffled friend little chance to explain or to counter specific accusations. John left the house quickly, more astonished than angry.

The Andersons' funds, the painfully saved dollars added to the remnants of the Doubleday-*Story* prize money, were almost gone. After a final session or two at the typewriter, Edward helped Anne put Helen in the gray Ford, and they headed toward Abilene while they still had enough money to buy nickel-a-gallon gas for the trip.

From here on out, Anderson would have to think entirely for himself, isolated from Knox's well-nourished and well-balanced intellect. John nursed no grudge, and would have gladly patched up the friendship, but although the emotional gap was small, the geographic one would soon become wide.

One day in downtown Abilene not long after the Andersons' return, Anne's brother and Edward were standing outside a store when they saw the familiar, large form of John Knox striding along the sidewalk some distance away.

Edward shook his head. "I don't know why I got so mad at old John," he said.

10. Radio Days in Denver

Edward and Anne were busted. They had almost no money left when they pulled into Abilene in the Ford. The car's gray steel body, once shiny, was now overlaid with road dust. Edward's literary career also lacked some of its former luster. Critics may have praised *Hungry Men,* but that did not mean book buyers had rushed to purchase the Doubleday trade edition that followed its Literary Guild edition for club members. Few first novels sell well. However, his New York agent had begun trotting the manuscript of his second novel around to publishers.

Edward and Anne and little Helen arrived at the white frame house at 1318 Jeanette, where Pearl Bates greeted them in the living room with the Axminster rug. Her son Luther was still living there also. The Anderson house wasn't even considered as a refuge. Anne still felt the Andersons were hostile to her, hadn't wanted her for an in-law, hadn't wanted to lose the only son in the family. When Ellen Anderson wanted to see her granddaughter, she would have to drive over to the Bates place on the south side.

Edward and Anne and Helen moved into Anne's old front bedroom with the rag rug. Anne's mother occupied the middle bedroom, and Luther the back bedroom. In the evenings, Anne and Edward could cool themselves in the swing on the front porch, which was festooned with honeysuckle.

Edward lost no time in making a visit to the *Abilene Reporter* and *Morning News* offices downtown. Was there an opening on the news staff, something on the desk maybe, even a simple reporting job? They shook his hand and congratulated him on his well-received hobo novel. Bernard Hanks, Frank Grimes, Max Bentley, and the others were proud

Sarah Ellen Sexton Anderson, Edward's mother

to have worked with him, although they would also feel a little of the envy that all newswriters experience when one of their number gets some prose enshrined between hard covers.

But there were no jobs at the *Reporter* or the *Morning News*. The management made do with a skeleton staff now, one reporter running around, waiting out the lean times, while the meager advertising sales staff cajoled even more meager two-by-four displays that barely kept the press rolling. No job, even for an internationally known novelist.

What about the WPA?

The WPA? Harry Hopkins's leaf rakers?

Why not? Hopkins's government agency had apparently figured out that writing was a kind of work. So they had come up with the WPA Writers' Project, which would produce guidebooks for each state. Edward was obviously a qualified, professional writer, and he was just as obviously out of work. So Edward went around to the other side of the block where the Works Progress Administration had its offices in the seven-story, red-brick Alexander Building. Winfred James (whose son Ted later became publisher of the *New York Daily News*) was WPA district manager. Edward signed on to write about the tourist sights in Abilene (alt. 1,719 ft., pop. 23,175) on Tour Number Ten in *Texas: A Guide to the Lone Star State*.

Edward wrote about such things as Abilene's polo team, noting that "the natty uniforms, scant saddlery, and thoroughbred horseflesh" typical of the game in the East were in West Texas replaced by "cowboy boots and big hats" and cow ponies. He roughed out a sketch of Abilene's early history and mentioned the high-school band, the three church-owned colleges, and the radio station, KRBC.

Anne, now obviously filling with their second child, drove Edward around in the gray Ford to such places as Fort Phantom Hill, where Robert E. Lee once kept an eye out for the Comanches, and Buffalo Gap, which had been the county seat until Abilene pirated the government and records a half century before and left only a tiny town with few persons and many trees. Edward also assigned Anne the job of keeping track of their mileage for the expense account, and she constantly mixed up the figures. At one ghost town they visited, Edward and Anne found only part of the one wall of a building standing. Through a paneless window in the wall, a stray donkey stuck his head to observe them.

The British reviews of *Hungry Men* had been the last to arrive, and in some ways they were even more encouraging than the American reviews. They had appeared mostly in the autumn of 1935 and were collected by the British clipping service, Durant's Press Cuttings, which shipped them to Anderson's publisher, who finally relayed them to Anderson.

Anne pasted the *Hungry Men* reviews in her scrapbook, but her enthusiasm was waning. Glamorous as literary acclaim might have initially appeared to her, she was beginning to wish she might make entries in the Anderson family bank book also. Her second child was due in August or perhaps September, and it cost money to bring babies into this world. About the only large asset that Edward and Anne owned that they might turn into money was the gray Ford.

American publishers had become cool to proletarian novels because those they had published in the first half of the thirties had not sold particularly well. Who would buy them? Not the rich, who hardly sympathized with the idea of an uprising of the have-nots. Not the have-nots, who had more important things to spend their money on. When they could spare two bits, they invested their coin in Hollywood-filmed fantasies. The few purchasers of proletarian novels were perhaps guilt-ridden, middle-class intellectuals flirting with fellow-travelerism. Such a slim audience could not mean healthy sales for a publishing house.

Fortunately for Edward Anderson, readers were still interested in the bandits who had freely raced around the nation's highways in the first half of the decade, until the police got radios in their cars and made such shenanigans more difficult. Although Alvin "Old Creepy Eyes" Karpis, the last of the mad-dogs, was taken alive, most of the stickup daredevils—John Dillinger, Clyde Barrow, Bonnie Parker, Pretty Boy Floyd, Baby Face Nelson, Raymond Hamilton, Ma Barker and her boys—had died violently and by doing so achieved a kind of inverse sainthood that long kept its hold on the popular imagination. There was even a traveling tent show featuring the bullet-riddled death-car and other relics of Bonnie and Clyde.

A much bigger show was the 1936 Texas Centennial celebration. Dallas was the center of the celebration, but its manifestations were everywhere. For instance, Gypsy Ted Sullivan Wylie—head of McMurry's art department, where Polly Anne had studied drawing and painting, had helped select a new state anthem:

Texas, our Texas
All hail the mighty state . . .

Just three years into this century, Texas governor Jim Hogg had suggested a Texas-size party to mark the San Jacinto victory that cut revolutionary Texas loose from Mexico. Hogg released the idea among
chauvinistic Texans where, like yeast in dough, it expanded and rose
for years. By the mid-twenties Texas possessed something called the
Centennial Governing Board of One Hundred. Then somebody discovered that the state constitution, written after the Civil War to hedge
against thieving carpetbaggers, forbade the use of state funds for a
centennial celebration. Texans passed a constitutional amendment in
1932 that would allow it. Finally, the legislature, after a great deal of
haggling, put up some money in 1934.

The fireworks and music were all around them, but Edward and
Anne had no time or money for such frills.

Edward's former friend J. Frank Dobie, however, was drawn against
his will into the literary facet of the party. When Dobie left Kerrville
in early 1936, he went to his friend Raymond Dickson's Caballo Ranch
in northern Mexico, where he sought even deeper solitude to write.
But before the year was out Dobie found himself ensnarled in the formation of the Texas Institute of Letters, which state literary figures
were forming under the aegis of the Centennial.

The idea for that parochial but useful regional writers' organization hatched in a 1935 statewide meeting of Sigma Tau Delta, the
English national honor society, at Mary Hardin Baylor College in Belton. Texans had long been conscious of having a distinct culture, different if not somehow superior to that of their fellow Americans. Their
Southern forebears had handed down to Texans the anti-intellectual
bias of the English upper class (captured wonderfully in the comic
novels of P. G. Wodehouse). What Texan wouldn't like to have a nickel
for every time he had heard a fellow Texan boast of his ignorance,
that he's "just a country boy and don't understand this high falootin'
stuff." Yet even Texas contained an intellectual community, small,
slightly ghettoized, slightly apologetic, and one that wrestled with problems of the mind, often while loudly proclaiming it preferred to watch
football or steer wrestling at the rodeo, preferred to hunt and fish,
preferred to swig beer and listen to string bands. By the thirties Texas
had produced several prose writers with national reputations. With

Dobie and Stanley Walker were Dorothy Scarborough, Eugene Cunningham, Barry Benefield, and Katherine Anne Porter, as well as such popular poets as Grace Noll Crowell and Karle Wilson Baker. A strong group of historians included Walter Prescott Webb, Rupert N. Richardson, J. Evetts Haley, and Eugene C. Barker. John A. Lomax was known nationally for his folk-song collecting. Texas even had a respectable literary magazine in the *Southwest Review*. The tumult of the Texas Centennial caused the state's writers to look around at one another and begin discussing some sort of organization.

Dobie missed the 1935 meeting at Belton, and he initially got involved by making fun of such a project. Like Lomax, Webb, and others, he found much in the idea to object to. Dobie looked over the proposed members and labeled one a "pedagogical nonentity" and another a "mere compiler." He was eventually talked around to becoming a supporter, however, and he was among the seventeen persons who attended the first meeting, on November 9, 1936, in the lecture room of the Hall of State at the Centennial Exposition in Dallas.

Anderson, completely cut off from Dobie, hadn't known of all this and wouldn't have cared if he had. He made no further ties with writers in his native Texas; his eyes were on wider horizons. He never worried about the political aspects of writing or kept up friendships for their own sake. He would never share a bottle and conversation with John Knox again. John wrote a letter or two, but Edward didn't answer.

Knox went his own way. It had been obvious to an observer such as Anne that John and Mabel Knox were mismatched. Sure enough, they drifted into separation and divorce. In the summer of 1939 John entered Southwestern General Hospital in El Paso to have his appendix removed. During his three days there, John got acquainted with a pretty nurse who had a soft Alabama voice. Her name was Elsie Lorene Oliver; she was a slender 5'7" and had golden brown hair. There were letters, dates. They were married March 24, 1941. They became parents of a twin son and daughter the following year, another daughter in 1943, and another son in 1950.

John worked for Bethlehem Steel in California during World War II. In June of 1945, the Knoxes moved to a farm at Devine, thirty miles from San Antonio, which John had bought at the suggestion of his father. He returned to writing pulp fiction, but by the fifties the pulps were dying. The Knox farmhouse burned in 1957, and although all the family escaped, John lost a novel he had nearly com-

pleted. While he was waiting for his daughter Jane to recover from
serious burns, John gave up booze forever. Two years later the Knoxes
moved to Mrs. Knox's home state, Alabama, settling in the Decatur
area, where John wrote features for the daily newspaper and eventually two books of local history, *A History of Morgan County*, published
in 1966, and *The Story of Decatur, Alabama* (with William H. Jenkins),
in 1970. John continued to sell occasional stories to national magazines.

With his poetry long behind him, his fiction career virtually closed,
John lived quietly with his wife Lorene in Hartselle, Alabama, where
they moved in 1978. He developed some property; he helped his oldest
son with building plans. He continued to satisfy his vast appetite for
books, reading history, philosophy, psychology, comparative religion,
and nuclear physics, and on pre-Columbian cultures. He told a friend
that "what excites me is the seeming convergence between ancient
sages and the modern pretzel-benders, a sort of shaking hands between Lao Tsu and Heisenberg, away out there where Nicholas of
Cusa detected his *coincidentia oppositorum* (or maybe it's just the spectre
of Spengler's 'second religiousness')." He made notes, but without any
real hope of developing them into a prose work: "A time comes when
a man should quit kidding himself." Near the end of his life in 1982,
the new scholarly edition of Proust appeared, and with delight Knox
reread *Remembrance of Things Past*.

In 1936 Anderson's Houston sweetheart, Melba Newton, married
a fellow journalist, Ernest H. Edinger, and became the mother of two
stepchildren. Melba was a good writer herself; the *Houston Post* bought
and serialized a novel by her. The Edingers moved to Richmond, Virginia, and she dropped "Melba" and began using her other given name,
Valerie. Ernest worked in public relations and development; Valerie
became women's editor of the *Richmond Times-Dispatch*.

Although he had lost touch with Melba Newton and—more important from a career standpoint—had cut himself off from both
Dobie and Knox, Anderson in 1936 was a lot more interested in his
financial situation. Busted. Anne and Edward stayed busted. They
got a trickle of cash for current bills from the WPA project, but not
enough to keep them from being broke. Anne could care for her daughter or sit in the living room of her mother's home and listen to "Amos
'n' Andy," or Kate Smith singing "When the Moon Comes over the
Mountain." Edward walked a good deal, energetically but aimlessly
and alone. Sometimes he walked to the Carnegie to check out books

from Maude Cole. Broke, another kid on the way, and no word from New York on *Thieves Like Us*. Edward would begin to wonder if he were going to have to get in the gray Ford and go hold up a bank himself.

He sent job-hunting letters to newspapers in the Southwest. From Denver, Colorado, where John Knox had so recently lived, Edward got an offer from the *Rocky Mountain News*. Texas flatlanders, with only the dwarfish tailings of the mighty Rockies in the state's far west, think of Denver as high, cool, and pleasant, a city in which to vacation. Edward eagerly accepted the offer. With Anne expecting their child, however, they decided that she should stay behind with her mother and continue under the care of her Abilene physician.

Not long after Anderson got to Denver, Brandt, and Brandt found a publisher, Frederick A. Stokes and Company, for his novel. A modest one-column headline in his Denver newspaper boasted "News Writer Will Publish Second Novel." The story says that Stokes describes the book as a "psychological study," one so original that Stokes was "anxious to bring it out when the gangster story as such is waning."

But back in Abilene, other matters were gaining the Anderson family's attention. The animosity between Edward's wife and his mother did not lessen. If Ellen Anderson wanted to see her first grandchild, her namesake, she still had to drive over and wait outside while Anne brought Helen out for her to see and hold. Ellen Anderson was a strong-minded woman who was not prone to changing her opinion once she had made up her mind; Anne's temper was hardly improved in those last days before labor. Dorothy Anderson and E. H. were more welcome over on Jeanette.

When her labor pains began in earnest, Anne called her sister Ruby to drive her to the hospital. Anne wanted to drop a suit of Edward's at the cleaners en route, and Ruby watched her go through its pockets. Anne discovered a letter. From another woman. It contained the sentence, "Oh, it was wonderful waking up to find your curly head on my pillow." The letter would give no peace to Anne's mind as Ruby steered down Hickory Street to Hendrick Memorial Hospital. A son arrived late on the night of August 20. Anne named him Dick Edward for his two grandfathers, and was always careful to remind officials filling out forms that it was Dick and not Richard.

Edward had not been working long on the *Rocky Mountain News*, but he had to see his new son. He took the first train home. To pay for the hospital expenses, Edward sold the gray Ford. There were lots of Fords around in 1936, and not much money; Edward and Anne had bought it for $800 a few months before, and now Edward sold it to the friend of a friend for $250.

The new father could stay only briefly before going back to the Rockies. Anne and the children would follow him to Colorado as soon as she and the new son were ready to travel.

Since Edward's father didn't drive a car, he would walk to the same place on the highway every day and wait until one of his many friends stopped to give him a lift to Merkel, where he worked at a print shop. E. H. Anderson called the little spot under a tree where he waited his "office." E. H. Anderson had a good sense of humor, and because of it his Merkel commuting arrangement was regarded not so much as an inconvenience as a source of laughter in his family. Louise Anderson once saw him arrive home in the sidecar of a motorcycle. On another occasion, he mentioned something he had told to a Los Angeles–bound stranger who took him to Merkel, and his wife pointed out that his information was wrong. "My God, mama," E. H. said, "now I'll have to go all the way to California to set that fellow straight."

Early one Saturday morning in September, a little over two weeks after the birth of his grandson, E. H. suddenly collapsed in his shade-tree office. The attendants at a nearby filling station saw him fall, rushed to investigate, and telephoned his wife. Louise was living in Ardmore at that time, working in a beauty shop owned by her aunt. Living at home were Dorothy, who was working as a stenographer, and Imogene, who had married longtime sweetheart Leon Hodges in December of 1935 but remained in Abilene to operate her dancing school while her husband completed his M.D. degree at Baylor Medical School in Dallas. The women came quickly in the family car to bring the fifty-nine-year-old printer home.

"Mama, this one is going to get me," E. H. told Ellen. Dr. William Snow, the regular family physician, was unavailable. Dr. L. F. "Slim" Johnson, two of whose daughters were dance pupils of Imogene, was summoned instead.

Medical science in 1936 had developed only three effective treatments for acute heart failure. The physician could bleed the patient, withdrawing a pint of blood to reduce the amount with which the heart had to cope. Or the physician could administer oxygen with a tent or tube, or inject digitalis, then available in a crude preparation of leaves, to strengthen the heart muscle. Dr. Johnson gave Anderson an injection.

E. H. lingered through the day. He died at six o'clock the following morning. Dorothy went over to Jeanette to tell Anne.

The funeral was held in an Abilene funeral home, in Laughter (the funeral director pronounced it "Law-ter") Chapel. Conducting the service was John's father, Dr. T. S. Knox, who presided over many rites of passage for the families of the little group of Abilene writers. Dr. E. B. Surface, pastor of Abilene's other Presbyterian church, shared duties as officiant. E. H. was officially a member of the Methodist Episcopal Church, South, but his Methodist ties had become very loose over the years and the family had begun attending Presbyterian services in Abilene.

Edward did not come home from Denver for his father's funeral; he had seen his father when he came home for the birth of his son just two weeks previously. Since his seniority at the Denver newspaper was so limited and jobs so scarce it would not have been a good idea to leave again and throw extra work on his colleagues too often. Seven hundred miles stretched between Denver and Abilene. Edward stayed put.

Anne caught the train to bring Helen Ann and Dick Edward to Denver in September of 1936. Edward installed the family in a two-story brick house just four doors off Colfax Avenue, a main thoroughfare leading to downtown Denver.

Soon after they got the family installed in the Denver house, an early snow fell, and catching the leaves still on many trees, it piled unusually high on tree branches, breaking many limbs, sometimes bringing down electrical lines with them. Anne liked to look out the second-story windows at the big brown squirrels, which climbed the trees and occasionally pattered across the roof of her house. They were much larger than the little gray squirrels to which she was accustomed.

Away from the newsroom, Edward's principal contribution to domestic chores was to keep everyone's shoes shined. Anne had discovered early in the marriage that she herself would have to repair screens and tinker with appliances because Edward, who was first rate in a newsroom or print shop, was definitely not a household handyman. Once Edward had decided to try to install a new washer to cure a leaking cold-water faucet. The operation was lit by a large white light fixture overhead. He locked his wrench around the pipe joint and yanked. The faucet came off and water spewed up in a powerful geyser, popping the light fixture. Anne came running in.

"You've got to turn off the water first," she shouted.

Edward grabbed the adjacent hot-water tap and tried to turn off his gusher with it. Anne finally got across the information that he would have to go outside and turn off all the water coming into the house.

With a toddler and a crib baby, Anne was kept at home much of the time, and getting out for shopping or errands was a treat. One day Anne caught a ten-cent streetcar down the nearby main drag to the newspaper office where Edward worked. She visited him briefly at his desk and got a good look at the place. She then decided to walk the seventeen blocks home for exercise. But it was colder than she thought, and by the time she arrived at the house, her feet were thoroughly chilled and she worried about bringing on a case of the grippe. But it didn't materialize.

To add to the family income, Edward began writing a radio show called *The Light of the West* for a Denver utility company. Edward dramatized regional history, poring over dusty records in the courthouse and elsewhere for material. He told Anne there were more stories in such archives than writers could ever use up. The half-hour shows aired once a week on radio station KOA.

One example of a typical Anderson radio show concerned the killing of a miner for the silver the victim had found. Edward found the ingredients of a detective story in the way the lawman deduced from a still ticking pocketwatch that its owner had not been missing for long. Then the body was discovered beneath the floorboards of his cabin.

Anderson had about eight radio actors at his disposal, and he tried to fit scripts to the strengths of his stock company. One actor had a magnificent voice. Edward wrote a play about a down-on-his-luck opera singer who got a job entertaining in a saloon and caused a riot when he cut loose with an aria. Often the dramatist looked in at the studio to see what the actors were doing with his lines. Now and then Anne went with him.

The income wasn't bad, and the Anderson family was getting along comfortably, but when the publisher's advance for *Thieves Like Us* arrived, Edward quit both the *Rocky Mountain News* and the radio drama. He wanted to write another novel, and he began as usual with a short but fairly elaborate narrative covering a good many pages, a narrative giving a bare outline of the story. The book was tentatively titled *Seven Hundred Wives* and concerned the American West in the nineteenth century.

It was then early 1937, and Robert Penn Warren was including Edward's short story, "The Guy in the Blue Overcoat," in his anthology, *Southern Harvest,* which also featured works by William Faulkner, Katherine Anne Porter, Erskine Caldwell, Allen Tate, John Peale Bishop, Marjorie Kinnan Rawlings, and Thomas Wolfe. When *Thieves Like Us* appeared to good reviews, Hollywood agent Adeline Schulberg contacted Edward to say that a scriptwriting job awaited him in the film capital. The previous year songwriters Cliff Friend and Dave Franklin had published a hit that Edward and Anne heard every time they twisted their radio dial: "When My Dreamboat Comes Home." Edward must have felt that his dreamboat had docked and that it only remained for him and Anne to get aboard.

11. Tinseltown

A porter at the Denver railway station observed a young couple seated in the waiting room one day. The man, in his early thirties, dressed in a business suit and tie, smoked a cigarette and talked in a low voice to his companion, a pretty young woman in her early twenties, simply but stylishly dressed, who seemed filled with sadness. Her nose was slightly pink and raw, hinting at recent weeping. Nothing odd about that, really; the porter had often seen mourners at the station, waiting to begin the melancholy journey home for a funeral. The jarring element was the man, who seemed curiously unsympathetic. Without raising his voice, the man made a quiet remark to the woman. Obviously hurt, Anne Anderson quit fighting back tears. Edward, wearing a long-suffering smile, glanced quickly around to see if anyone was watching. A discreet porter always managed to be looking elsewhere in such a situation.

The Andersons were headed for Hollywood, where Edward would try his hand at writing for motion pictures. In the thirties Hollywood was perceived as the magic abode of princesses such as Shirley Ross, heroes such as John Barrymore, sirens such as Mae West, villains such as Edward G. Robinson. Writers went there as much to be amazed as to collect huge paychecks for putting words into the mouths of the silver screen's stars.

When Adeline Schulberg read *Thieves Like Us* and loved it, she contacted Anderson and urged him to come out to the West Coast, where she would arrange for him to make big money writing for a film studio. Ad Schulberg had been married to producer B. P. Schulberg, but when the marriage broke up, she went out and became a successful Hollywood agent, a career overwhelmingly pursued by males at that time.

Edward eagerly looked forward to invading Movieland. He wanted to explore its wonders with Anne, but he also felt that they should not drag along two small children. They should be able to waltz onto the scene as lightly as Fred and Ginger.

Anne's feelings were mixed. Since she had become Edward's wife, Anne had seen New Orleans celebrate Mardi Gras, helped Edward write an internationally acclaimed novel, and witnessed the creation of broadcasts when radio was one of the most popular forms of home entertainment. Now, Hollywood! But during those two years with Edward, Anne had become the mother of little Helen Ann and Dick Edward. She was thinking that it would be more interesting to watch her child learn to walk and talk than to see the movie stars. Yet there was the letter she had found in Edward's suit right before Dick Edward was born.

Moving and setting up housekeeping was no problem; the Andersons had been renting a furnished house in Denver, and they had acquired few possessions aside from the children. Edward was adamant about not taking the children. So reluctantly, Anne wrote to her mother. Pearl Bates got her son Luther to drive her to Denver, and they returned to Abilene with the grandchildren. Helen would stay with Anne's sister Ruby and Dick Edward with Pearl.

When Pearl and Luther had taken the children away, Anne sank into melancholy. Since her husband was so much older and more experienced, Anne thought she should not argue with his decisions, but her squelched feelings found less direct ways of expressing themselves: Anne had fits of crying, and her digestive system protested. Edward had fantasized about making love with Anne in the cozy privacy of a Pullman berth, while the car swayed and its metal wheels whirled over the railed miles spanning Utah, Nevada, and Arizona. Not a chance. It simply wasn't possible with the disconsolate Anne having indigestion and sniffles. In the most famous movie fantasy of the thirties, Dorothy locked arms with the Scarecrow, the Tin Woodman, and the Lion to skip along the yellow-brick road into the Emerald City with a dream in her heart, a Harold Arlen tune on her lips, and Toto at her heels. Edward and the gloomy Anne didn't even have a dog at their heels when they hit Los Angeles.

At the Los Angeles station, the Andersons were met by Ad Schulberg and her daughter Sonya. Ad was an attractive middle-aged woman with expressive eyes and a full-lipped mouth often pulled back in a smile. The agent knew the value of a buck; she was a thoroughly civilized woman as well. As they went to claim the Andersons' luggage, Edward listened to Ad and her daughter argue about the pronunciation of the word "vase"—should it rhyme with "chase," or should it be "vahze," to rhyme with "bahs"? (Only a half century later would Anne know the true answer: It rhymed with "chase" if it cost less than fifty dollars, and it was "vahze" if it cost more.)

The job worried Edward more than proper pronunciation did, and he asked if it were nailed down tight. Well, that isn't exactly the way it's done out here in Hollywood. Ad had arranged a series of interviews at the studios. Instead of simply shaking hands with a new boss and hanging up his hat, Edward would have to make a round of question-and-answer meetings during the next few days, a painful process for a man who was basically shy.

After a night of uneasy sleep, Edward marched off to parade his accomplishments. B. P. Schulberg at Paramount finally hired him, and Edward took the good news home to Anne. Anne was having her own problem trying not to mope; the little efficiency apartment they had rented overlooked a school playground, and the sight of the children constantly called her own faraway babes to mind.

So Edward went to work for Ben P. Schulberg, slender and silver-haired, with a cigar in his mouth, producer of hundreds of motion pictures. As a young man in New York, Schulberg himself had worked on newspapers and magazines before quitting journalism to write publicity and scenarios for the great Edwin S. Porter, who had put together the first American films with genuine stories—*The Life of an American Fireman* and *The Great Train Robbery*. By the time Edward began work for Schulberg, B. P. had slipped from his position as head of production at Paramount, but he continued to create movies in association with the company.

Schulberg installed Edward in the office just vacated by William Saroyan. Like Anderson, Saroyan was a discovery of *Story* magazine. Martha Foley and Whit Burnett had accepted Saroyan's "The Daring Young Man on the Flying Trapeze" for *Story*'s issue of February, 1934, and this short fiction in turn became the title work in the Armenian-American's first book, a volume also published in 1934 and one that generated much critical praise. Schulberg had hired Saroyan in 1936 at a weekly salary of three hundred dollars, double the amount Anderson was glad to get a year later.

Edward and Anne in Southern California

Saroyan's fiction was generally best when the author was speaking in his own voice, as he did in his often-anthologized story, "Seventy Thousand Assyrians." In Hollywood he did not succeed in creating dialogue in a sufficiently disciplined script to please Paramount story editor George Auerbach and Schulberg. So he left (commenting sourly on the experience forty years later in his curious book *Obituaries,* a rambling collection of informal, acid "obituaries" of people he had known). Saroyan went to New York, where he continued struggling with dialogue by writing a series of plays that attracted a good deal of interest but had spotty financial success on Broadway. The most popular of these was *The Time of Your Life,* the five acts of which Saroyan wrote in five days, "a good week's work," as he put it.

Edward's personality would seem pale to Schulberg after that of the eccentric, prose-gushing Saroyan, but his dialogue in *Hungry Men* and *Thieves Like Us* possessed a hard, clear realism. It promised Schulberg relief from Saroyan's dialogue, in which the masks of the various characters barely hid the features of Saroyan's own hyperactive ego.

George Auerbach was a nut about college football. The prolific Saroyan had hatched a story about a varsity gridder, under the working title *An American Hero.* After his college playing days, the hero fails

at legitimate enterprises in the big world, turns to crime, and winds
up trying to escape the police, running for dear life one night down
a darkened football field.

After installing Edward in Saroyan's old office, Schulberg handed
him the *American Hero* story to turn into a screenplay. Anderson sat
down at the desk with no more knowledge of the procedures of motion-
picture writing than he had of the geography of the other side of the
moon. But he was confident. In the past seven years he had wrestled
with the rules for writing pulp fiction, serious novels, and true detectives. Anderson now set himself to master this new technique of dramatic writing, with its jungle of cant terms: *closeup, three shot, fade in.* . . .

In his spare time, Edward, to get his mind off the puzzles of screenwriting, liked to go down to the gym and watch the boxers work out.
Anne at first went with him. They got acquainted with some of the
fighters and managers. The novelty of watching young gladiators pound
punching bags, or one another's heads, soon dimmed for Anne, and
Edward noticed that she seemed increasingly blue. Near the Andersons' efficiency apartment was an ice rink, a great palace with a vast
floor of frozen liquid. Trying now to get Anne's mind off her faraway
kids, Edward took her to a skating review there, a colorful production
with stage lovers dancing in tandem, clowns, an orchestra sawing its
way through the likes of "Blue Danube" and "The Merry-Go-Round
Broke Down." Anne's mind warmed to the spectacle, even as she felt
the cold creep out of the arena and up her legs, down her collar, up
her sleeves.

The floor to their apartment might as well have been ice too, as
long as its window overlooked that playground. Edward reluctantly
left Anne for work each morning. He knew that every time she heard
and saw the schoolchildren, she was tortured with thoughts of their
son and daughter. A firm believer in exercise (he still managed to take
long walks and play tennis), Edward suggested that Anne try to learn
to ice skate herself. Anne went over to the ice palace during the day,
strapped on some blades, and slid awkwardly out on the floor. American towns of the twenties all were equipped with sidewalks, and as
a child Anne had rollerskated over miles of them in San Angelo, El
Paso, Houston, and Fort Worth. Now she mastered ice skating, but
she couldn't enjoy it somehow. Her ankles turned in. She still cried
a lot in the solitude of the apartment, and her indigestion persisted.

Edward in Hollywood, where he played tennis to stay in shape

She would switch on the radio, and an orchestra would be playing Hawaiian music—she detested Hawaiian music.

Then one morning Edward and Anne discovered that Sonja Henie was rehearsing in the ice palace. At twenty-four Henie was just two years older than Anne, yet she had won her first world's figure-skating championship a decade earlier in Oslo, Norway, had won three gold medals in three Olympics, and in 1937 was making her first (and ultimately biggest) cinema splash with her debut films, *One in a Million* and *Second Fiddle*. The exhibitors enjoyed packed theaters. The press called her the "Pavlova of the Ice." If the critics grumbled a little because she couldn't act, nobody else cared.

So while Edward went back to the strange world of the studio, Anne walked over to the rink and went in to watch the rehearsal. Nobody much was there, a scattered few onlookers who glanced at her without much interest as she sat down.

Then Henie entered. She was smaller than Anne expected, only 5'2", but her 110 pounds was all graceful muscle and bone, like a ballerina; she had studied dance under Madame Karsavina in London. Her legs had become famous when she had shocked and pleased judges in 1927 by appearing in "a dazzling white silk and ermine costume with very abbreviated skirt." In these heady days of Hollywood, Henie had insured her legs with the largest amount that Lloyd's of London would underwrite: five thousand dollars a week.

With Sonja Henie came a host of coaches, studio persons, hangers-on, and flunkies. She was a perfectionist. When she had won only third place in the 1924 Olympic tryouts, Henie had begun practicing seven hours a day, and since Norway had no indoor rinks, she had traveled to Germany, England, Switzerland, and Austria in order to skate the year round.

Anne waited with interest to see what this sylphlike being would do. Almost immediately Henie began to shout at the persons with her, like a drill sergeant would. Anne had expected Henie's drive for perfection but not her tone of voice. A run-through began, and Henie floated out on the shimmering surface of the rink, a fairy queen in ethereal flight. Then she missed a turn, and Anne watched as Henie's highly insured buttocks slammed down on the ice. Now Anne witnessed a real display of Henie's temper. The handful of onlookers were glimpsing the tough reality behind the clever dialogue and sentimental songs that mesmerized audiences in movie houses around the globe. A disillusioned Anne withdrew. She had seen all the Hollywood glamour she cared to that day.

At 8:40 in the morning, Edward Anderson passed beneath the arched *Paramount* sign to enter the studio grounds. He opened the door to the writers' building and strode down the long hallway to the monastic little cubicle — it reminded him of a cell in a beehive — which had been assigned as his office. By 9:00 he had lit a cigarette and was pondering how to handle a sequence in *An American Hero*.

Long before sound joined sight in the film industry's products, the pecking order among writers had been established. Those making $2,000 per week might arrive at the studio as late as 11:00 A.M., or even not arrive at all if they preferred to write at home. Those salaried at

$500 to $1,500 were expected to show up by 10:00 at the latest. Those working for $350 could dally till 9:30 A.M., but junior writers were expected at 9:00 sharp.

Edward earned $150 a week. This was roughly six times what he might have earned on a Texas newspaper, where, if it happened to be an afternoon paper, the managing editor would demand that he show up for work around, say, 6:45 in the morning. When he compared it to newspapering, Edward would feel that in coming to Hollywood he had signed on as a deck hand for the good ship Lollipop.

Although Saroyan, who had cobbled together the plot on which Edward was working that morning, had been paid twice Edward's salary, both of them worked for peanuts by Hollywood standards. What producer would make a major film from a script written by such pikers? Major films were shot from expensive scripts written by high-priced geniuses who drew maybe $5,200 per week, like the team of Dorothy Parker and her new husband, Alan Campbell. Screenwriters of the era have written that bosses, in all times and in all places, value most highly the stuff that costs them the most. Why, if a $150-a-week writer did write a scene or two worth using, chances were that his producer would add a half dozen adjectives and pirate the screen credit.

Edward hammered away at his typewriter keyboard. He lit more cigarettes. The sequence was taking shape. *Two shot. Tracking shot. Fade out.* Around ten o'clock, he hit a snag. Deep in thought, he opened a drawer in his desk to take out the crackers, onion, and tomato juice that was still his preferred snack. He sampled them while he read over his morning's work. A way of overcoming the difficulty would come to him, and after returning the food to its drawer, he began rewriting his last page.

By noon he had run dry of ideas, and Edward emerged from his office at the same time George Auerbach was coming out of his adjacent office with Ted Auerbach, his brother. George said something disparaging about the weather; he was a small man with bright eyes, and he seldom made a complimentary remark.

In the commissary Edward paid scant attention to his meal or to the famous faces in the room. He read a book as he ate. When he had first come to Paramount, Edward was dazzled by celebrities, but he quickly became accustomed to recognizing Randolph Scott or Lew Ayres, Carole Lombard or Ida Lupino in the commissary or around the lot, all of them, like himself, under contract to Paramount.

Words did not flow so easily after lunch. Edward was glad when Anne, out in town for some shopping, turned up in midafternoon. They talked, and at odd moments she hummed snatches of a recent tune, "Smoke Gets in Your Eyes." Although it had a great Jerome Kern melody, its appeal for Anne was in the bittersweet Otto Harbach words—a torch singer, usually female, lamenting that her heart had blinded her to the faults of her sweetheart, faults she recognized later through her tears.

Why, Anne asked Edward, hadn't this wonderful song climbed to the top of the music chart?

Edward, whose musical preferences ran more to Jimmie Rodgers strumming "Any Old Time," smiled his sardonic smile and suggested she ask George Auerbach.

To think was to act with a girl who had adopted Pollyanna's name. She clicked her heels right down the hall to Auerbach's office, where she found George and Ted. Whatever George's train of thought, Anne interrupted it with her question about "Smoke Gets in Your Eyes."

George studied her with unclouded eyes. If he had asked, Anne herself would have had difficulty explaining just why the song appealed to her, its words perhaps touching knowledge Anne kept pushed back into her subconscious. Oh, Auerbach only said, it'll be up there. It'll be up there.

When he took Anne to the movies, Edward watched with a critical eye. He read movie screenplays, he visited sets to observe how movies were made. Anne was curious about all this too, and one day in the fall of 1937 she drove up to the Paramount gate. When Cary Grant or Marlene Dietrich drove up to the arched studio gate, they were waved through with a smile. Not so most folks. A great army of rubbernecking tourists infested the streets of Burbank and Hollywood, on foot, in cars, packing sightseeing buses. Many Los Angeles area residents were just as curious; finally, Central Casting in 1937 listed 15,000 bit players called "extras," of whom 14,599 dreamed of riveting the attention of someone with the power to offer a real speaking-part studio contract. The movie makers couldn't afford to let these curious and ambitious mobs in. To have opened the studio gates would have halted production and turned Paramount into a forerunner of Disneyland. So, when Anne drove up, the guard took a hard-eyed look at Anne's identification before smiling and letting her through. Edward, who had arranged for her to get in, was waiting, and they walked over to the set where director Mitch Leison was filming *The Big Broadcast of 1938,* a frothy concoction with almost no story (Bob Hope claimed that *Variety* once offered ten thousand dollars to anyone who could tell the film's plot) in spite of, or perhaps because of, five writers listed in the credits.

Edward and Anne joined the group who watched from behind cameraman Harry Fishbeck. They had happened on an outdoor scene, but it was being filmed inside a studio where the artificial sunlight was under the absolute control of technicians.

Shirley Ross was in front of the camera. The actress was Anne's age, and she sang, danced a little, and even played the piano some while she was a student at UCLA. Anne was surprised to see that the slender Ross was a rather plain girl with a long nose.

Big Broadcast would launch the careers of both Ross and the young Broadway comedian named Bob Hope. In it they sang a duet written by Leo Robin and Ralph Rainger entitled "Thanks for the Memory." Ross, playing one of the Hope character's three ex-wives, reminisced musically with him about better days. "Thanks for the Memory" would become a big moment professionally for both of them. For Hope it became the foundation for a half century of national stardom; he adopted "Thanks" as his personal theme song. It placed Ross on a career plateau that eroded by the mid-forties. Ross frequently was a guest on other stars' radio shows, and she would invariably be asked to sing "Thanks for the Memory." All this, however, was still in the lockbox of time when Edward and Anne watched Leison directing Ross in the scene shot that day in 1937.

Ross was seated. They photographed her, but her dress wasn't quite right. An assistant rushed forward to draw the hem a little higher. They photographed her again, and this time her hair wasn't in the proper place, and again an assistant rushed forward. Edward and Anne watched as Ross, Fishbeck, Leison, and a battalion of helpers edged painstakingly toward a few feet of perfect film that might well be cut and discarded eventually.

Anne, stifling her impulse to ask questions aloud, took in every move, every thread, every curl. She would never again see a movie without wondering just where the lights were placed. Edward watched how every inch of celluloid was molded by the director with as much care as he himself molded each individual sentence. He realized again that this kind of storytelling was shaped as much by the producer, the director, and the camera operator as it was by the screenwriter.

At Paramount or around town, Edward impressed many who met him as being self-controlled, reserved in manner, and laconic in speech. But his behavior masked real shyness. Anne was the talker of the pair. Once the Andersons were at the famous Grauman's Chinese Theatre, the scene of so many spectacular motion picture premieres during the thirties, when Johnny Weissmuller was standing out front in his Tarzan costume. It was a warm day fortunately because a lot of the former swimming champ, tanned and muscular, showed outside his king-of-the-jungle loincloth. Most of the crowd gawked happily, delighted to find themselves backstage at fantasyland. One little girl, however, took a single look and began to sob. Seeing her predicament, Anne took the child by the hand and gently led her to Weissmuller, who bent over to bring his smiling face down to the little girl's level. Her tears forgotten, replaced with curiosity, the girl decided Tarzan wasn't such a bad fellow after all. At a deep level Edward too was panicked by many of the strange fish he encountered in the movie world, panicked into a frozen shyness. Anne was forever taking him by the hand also and leading him up to friendly strangers. Edward didn't like Anne taking the child up to Weissmuller that day; he told her that she had made a spectacle of herself.

On another occasion, the Andersons got ready to go to B. P. Schulberg's home. Schulberg had invited them to a party at the house that his novelist son Budd called "a pseudo-Spanish castle of white stucco on Benedict Canyon." Edward accepted Hollywood party invitations, and despite his shyness, made himself go because of Anne and because of his own curiosity about the high life. Yet he was so ill at ease there that he sometimes almost lost his voice. Edward put on a clean shirt, lit a cigarette, and thought he was fooling Anne by remaining deadpan. He was drinking more lately. She observed that he had a couple of drinks before they left for Schulberg's castle.

Anne enjoyed parties; she talked to everyone. At this gathering Anne met B. P. Schulberg, a distinguished-looking man of medium height, with graying hair and a long, aristocratic nose, and the masterful ease of a person accustomed to authority. Ben Schulberg probably was not reminded of Sylvia Sidney by Anne's eyes because Schulberg knew Sylvia Sidney all too well. Schulberg had pursued a long love affair

Edward meets FBI chief J. Edgar Hoover in California

with her in the early thirties, an affair that ultimately broke up his marriage of more than two decades to Adeline. He had had affairs with many actresses, including his own discovery, Clara Bow, the "It Girl" of the twenties.

Edward was less ill at ease at parties in this house than at others. Ben Schulberg, who always thought of himself as a writer, filled his parties with them. The Andersons found themselves in a house that pulsed with laughter, with talk of books and writing, with straight banter interrupted by stiff drinks.

Anne and Edward were introduced to Budd Schulberg, the oldest of the producer's three children. Budd was quite interested in Edward; he was interested in all writers. Although in the late thirties he was serving an apprenticeship in the movie business first with David Selz-nick and later with Walter Wanger, Budd was already simmering the ingredients of *What Makes Sammy Run?*, his famous 1940 novel. Anne, who didn't realize that she was just a year younger than Budd, thought he looked hardly grown up, with a youthful grin and a mass of curly hair. She found him an extremely handsome young man.

Talking with Edward, Budd would quickly discern that this diffi-dent writer from Abilene, Texas, lacked the brassy push of Sammy Glick, the character he created for his novel. Whatever Edward's tal-ent, he would need a whole lot of luck on the West Coast if he lacked "Glickishness"—singlemindedness and a tiger's instinct for survival in the Hollywood jungle.

One morning at breakfast in their apartment, Edward and Anne were finishing the remnants of toast and the morning newspaper when a photograph on an inside page jabbed Anne's memory. It pictured a hefty young woman seated in front of a typewriter.

"That's Dora Fallon!"

Anne's exclamation meant nothing to Edward. He had no recollec-tion of the round-faced coed with whom Anne had attended John Knox's poetry reading, where she caught her first glimpse of Edward, almost four years earlier.

The newspaper said the young woman could not remember who she was or where she came from. Somebody had noticed her sitting distractedly on a park bench. She had not eaten for three days. Al-though she couldn't play two notes of music when they set her in front of a piano, a typewriter was a different matter: She typed rapidly and accurately.

Edward and Anne hurriedly finished dressing. When Edward was shaved and Anne made up, they caught a taxicab to the place where the unidentified girl was sheltered. Officials welcomed the Andersons, who were precisely the sort of respondents they had hoped for when they released the picture. Anne gave them the name of Dora's family. Since she didn't know any address except Abilene, they phoned the police in Abilene and asked them to find the Fallon family.

Perhaps if Edward and Anne took Dora with them for the after-noon, Dora might remember a familiar face, the familiar West Texas twangs. Anne was shocked by the condition of her old friend. Dora had been a substantial girl in college, but now she was genuinely fat. Her hair was greasy, and she was unwashed and generally neglected.

The Andersons took her back to their apartment, but Dora remained shy and confused. Edward would look on Dora's vague condition with the mildly cynical amusement of a journalist, but Anne found it scary.

Anne asked Dora if she could remember McMurry College. Dora could, after a fashion, recall some kind of a campus, but it had no more substance for her than the flickering of dreams. She could not remember the mock Greek columns on the face of the three-story administration building, nor the art and choral teacher with the wonderful name, Gypsy Ted Sullivan Wylie, conducting the McMurry Chanters in "O God, Our Help in Ages Past," nor John Knox reading his sonnet about Fort Phantom Hill to Julia Luker's English class. At the end of the afternoon Edward and Anne took Dora back to the psychologists and told them that Dora's memory was still a blur.

Clay Fallon, who worked in the oil industry, rode the bus a thousand miles from Abilene to Los Angeles to reclaim his daughter. He told the Andersons only that Dora had been en route to El Paso when she disappeared, so the Andersons remained mystified. Fallon and Dora closed this curious incident for the Andersons by boarding the bus to begin the long, long trip home. The Fallons soon moved from Abilene, and Anne and Edward heard no more of Dora. It was as though a careless bookbinder had inserted a chapter from somebody else's novel into the story of the Andersons.

At another party one evening Edward and Anne ran into the legendary writer and critic Dorothy Parker. Anne was seized with an almost instant dislike for Parker, because the author of the line "men seldom make passes at girls who wear glasses" was herself nearsighted and her strange method of compensating was, when introduced, to lean forward and closely examine Anne and Edward in turn, beginning about knee-level and sweeping upward to their foreheads. The fact was that Parker squinted at everybody she met in similar fashion, but that didn't salve Anne's feelings about such rude treatment.

Although shy in the midst of the party crowd, Edward rediscovered his old skill with individual women as he held an impromptu tête-à-tête with Parker. They hit it off beautifully. Parker would find Edward more than handsome enough, and thoroughly interesting once he began to talk. Others at the party must have been puzzled by the friendship that had sprung up between Anderson, the provincial tough-guy novelist, and Parker, the sophisticated New York writer with the wit as keen as a hornet sting.

They had certain ideas in common: sympathy for the common people and an interest in possible radical solutions to the agony of the Depression, ideas implicit in the hard, naturalistic prose of Anderson's novels and stories. Parker was calling herself a communist in the late thirties, although it was really more a matter of sympathy for the underdog than a methodical, deliberate adoption of Marxist beliefs. She had not gone hungry and ridden boxcars as Anderson had, but she had gone to Spain to write about the Loyalist cause, and she had walked out of a restaurant at the Waldorf-Astoria Hotel in a show of support for striking waiters.

More important in the success of their instant rapport, however, was that Anderson and Parker were both shy. She hated the feeling that, once introduced to someone at a party, she was expected to begin spouting epigrams and memorable one-liners. Edward did not push Dorothy to be funny. In *Hungry Men,* Anderson had used Corinne's taste for Dorothy Parker's verse as a broad hint that that Corinne was intellectually shallow, but in reality he respected Parker's crisp, ironic short stories. Dorothy had once described herself as "just a little Jewish girl trying to be cute," but Edward didn't pressure her to be cute either.

Anne, watching the two writers absorbed in conversation, tried not to glare at them from across the room, but her green eyes grew greener with jealousy. Parker's husband, screenwriter Alan Campbell, wasn't at the party. When Dorothy decided it was time to leave, Edward helped her into her coat. Anne, trying to make small talk with another group of guests, watched out of the corner of her eye, dying of jealousy and despising the ridiculous pointed hat on the woman's head.

Edward Anderson's contract with Schulberg at Paramount was almost up, and the studio seemed to have no intention of turning a crank on his script for *An American Hero* in the near future, perhaps ever. Some very able writers — F. Scott Fitzgerald and Anthony Powell, to name only two — never managed to get a single Hollywood screenwriting credit. Anderson, without such a credit, knew he would probably not get his contract renewed by Paramount, and he might even have a difficult time catching on with another studio.

Edward and Anne dropped by the house that George Auerbach shared with his brother Ted. Edward's expiring contract preyed on his mind; he wanted to sound the story editor on his chances of renewal. After the group seated themselves in the Auerbach living room,

George's twelve-year-old Scottie dog limped in on three legs. Anne asked what was wrong with the dog.

Oh, Scotties just do that, Auerbach replied. He's old, He's worn out, and. . . .

Edward could see that Anne didn't like this flippant way of treating the dog's ailment. He picked up the conversation and moved it away from dogs. After a while Edward asked George point-blank what he thought of chances for renewal of Edward's contract.

"You never had a chance," Auerbach said. "It's because you came in the back door."

What did he mean by that? Edward later explained to Anne that he had been hired at Paramount because Adeline Schulberg, as B. P.'s ex-wife, had the connections there. At the end of his contract, Edward found himself once again looking for a job.

12. Warner Brothers

On a sunny day in 1938, a familiar gray Buick moved slowly down a street in Burbank, California, the big, muscular man who drove trying to help the older woman in the passenger seat read off the house numbers. In the backseat were a tired and excited three-year-old girl and two-year-boy. Pearl Bates said, there it is, Son. Luther Bates steered the heavy car into the driveway and braked.

Anne Anderson hurried out the door of the stucco bungalow to greet little Helen and Dick Edward, and when that was done, to greet her mother and brother. Although the depression had lowered the American birth rate, Anne had seemed to see children everywhere, painfully reminding her of her own back in Abilene. Now that anguish was over and done with.

Edward, smiling and sober as a Sunday school teacher, came along behind Anne. He spoke to his mother-in-law, shook hands with the huge Luther, hugged the children.

The Bateses, mother and son, had come to California to stay, Pearl having sold the house on Jeanette, thus cutting Anne's strongest tie with Texas. Of the Bates family, only Luther's twin sister was still in Abilene. Edward's mother and sisters remained in Abilene, but he had little contact with them; he never wrote them, and long-distance telephone calls for most people in the 1930s were to deliver death messages and the like. Pearl and Luther would put up at the Andersons until they could find quarters of their own, and Luther would have to look for a job. But first they all settled in to listen to the radio. Edward in particular, veteran newsman that he was, needed to hear the news for his daily ration of violence and catastrophe.

Edward and Helen in Los Angeles

The popular music on the air in 1938 included "Jeepers Creepers" and "I've got a Pocketful of Dreams," but the tunes preceded somber news broadcasts for men still below the maximum age for military conscription, such as Luther, thirty-one, and Edward, thirty-three. Italy had already gobbled up Abyssinia, Japan was pushing farther into China, Germany had swallowed Austria, and Italy and Germany were openly helping Franco to throttle the Spanish republic. There was little good news on the air that evening for the Andersons and Bateses to talk about, so they began to bring one another up to date. Edward had left Paramount at the end of his contract period, but he soon caught on with Warner Brothers. He and Anne had moved out to Burbank to be near Warners' Studio. Although he didn't bring any Paramount screen credits with him, he had learned a great deal about screenwriting and about the motion-picture business.

Warners seemed better suited to Anderson's type of writing. Even Pearl and Luther back in Abilene had been aware of the Warner reputation for bare-knuckled realism. Although it was Paramount that had triggered the wave of gangster films with *Underworld,* starring George Bancroft, in 1927, by 1938 it was Warners who maintained in its contract repertory company Hollywood's most celebrated mob of tough cookies: Edward G. Robinson, James Cagney, Humphrey Bogart, and John Garfield. The studio attracted writers on the order of John Bright, who paid little attention to Hollywood's nightclubs and parties as subject matter, instead watching the odd creatures of the Los Angeles streets: the demi-virgin who would do anything to keep eating between calls from Central Casting, the legless WWI vet who sold apples, the street preacher, the dope peddler, the drunk, the shoeshine boy. Such writers cranked out many first-rate slices of realism, in spite of the fact that Jack Warner had characterized all writers as "schmucks with Underwoods."

Jack Warner often seemed as tough and crude as any of the hoodlum characters played by Cagney, Bogart, and Robinson. He demanded that Edward and all the rest of his writers arrive at the writers' building at 8:30 each morning, break only an hour for lunch, and not leave before 5:30 in the afternoon. Six days a week, Monday through Saturday. Warner expected Edward to crank out twenty to thirty pages of screenplay every day. There was even a trench dug around the writers' building, so that nobody could sneak away from the typewriter and into the wilds of Burbank. The studio security guard, Blayney

Edward in his office at Warner Brothers

Mathews, sometimes hid out on a nearby roof to see who was dodging out for coffee at the drugstore across the street.

Whereas Paramount's Ben Schulberg was a real writer's producer who could see the dramatist possibilities in, say, a young Bill Saroyan, who had written only such arty stories as "Seventy Thousand Assyrians," Jack Warner thought of himself as a showman. He began his career as a singer and motion-picture projectionist and seldom aspired to write anything more extended than a payroll check, and his talent with check writing was for understatement. Even so, Warner checks still beat the wages paid by newspapers; Warner Brothers paid writers from $75 a week all the way up to $1,750. Yet the studio frequently fired writers when their options expired, to avoid giving them the raises specified for contract renewal. They'd be fired and then rehired a few days later at the old wage.

Jack Warner or not, the writers whom Edward joined still thought of themselves as the intellectual elite of the studio. They kept to themselves at their own table during lunch at the Warners commissary, which was called the "Greenroom." Producers, directors, and actors were excluded from the writers' table, but occasionally the thirty-five

Warners writers broke ranks to let a pretty actress sit with them. Although Edward enjoyed the talk of his colleagues, putting in his two cents in his quiet and cynical way, his loner inclination would ultimately make him uncomfortable with all the camaraderie and collaboration that is part of theatrical enterprises.

The studio commissaries would give Edward some interesting glances into the behavior of the famous, first at Paramount and then at Warners, and he made an attempt to share some of these wonders with Anne by taking her to lunch at one of the three Brown Derby restaurants in the film capital. Shaped like an enormous derby, each of the restaurants sported a neon sign on its crown saying, "Eat in the Hat." Since the original Brown Derby opened across from the Ambassador Hotel in 1926, the three hat-shaped restaurants had operated as sort of open clubs for the show-business community. There Anne could see not only stars but the character actors whose faces appeared in film after film and whose names appeared steadily (if in somewhat smaller type) in the credits, faces with names like Frank McHugh and Frank Morgan.

On one visit to the Derby, Anne and Edward picked up an acquaintance with another Edward who sometimes played mobsters and heavies — big, smiling Edward Arnold. Six years earlier Arnold had made the transition from a successful stage to a successful movie career with roles in *Okay America* at Universal and in *Rasputin and the Empress* at MGM, where he would act under contract for most of his career. At about the time the Andersons met him, he was on the nation's movie screens playing Achille Weber in *Idiot's Delight.*

Arnold, on a table-hopping expedition, sat down with the Andersons. They introduced themselves, and Arnold decided this table with the laconic man and his pretty, talkative wife would be a pleasant place to eat. The Andersons had ordered earlier, and now Arnold gave his order to the young waitress, who wore a flared, derby-shaped skirt that was the Derby livery.

The two Edwards and Anne talked, pleasantly. An Arnold acquaintance went by.

"Shalom," said Arnold.

From this, Anne jumped to the silent, and incorrect, conclusion that Arnold — who had grown up a Lutheran — was Jewish. And when the food came, Anne was surprised to see the great actor eating asparagus with his fingers.

Hollywood, Hollywood! Edward would note with satisfaction that his wife, so often discontented these days, was amused and thoroughly interested.

Anne visited Edward now and then at his office at Warners, although with her daughter and son now in their house she had less time to explore the movie studio. During one visit with Edward at the writers' building, Anne fell into conversation with Sydelle Tarshis, Edward's secretary, and Anne casually invited her to come by the house. To Anne's surprise, Sydelle did come by. The visits between the two women continued, multiplied. They talked together, and even cooked together; Sydelle taught Anne to make Jewish dishes and to savor matzo crackers. Anne had found her first real woman friend since coming to California. Edward would be glad to see his wife have a friend, a development that made life at home more relaxed.

At his desk, facing his Underwood, Edward found that motion-picture writing still eluded him the way pulp-magazine writing had eluded him. The reason was much the same: 95 percent of all movies made in the thirties, like the pulp stories from which they so often had been taken, were based on formulas that had continued to sell tickets since the days of the silents. The movie moguls reasoned that when a poor man or woman plunked down twenty-five or thirty-five cents for a ticket, he or she trusted the studio to deliver the kind of flickering dream he or she had enjoyed before and wished to enjoy again. In Hollywood, the producers suggested the ideas to the writers, and at Warners even those ideas were restricted to certain topic areas: Action, Africa, Biography, Costume, Gangster, Industrial, Mystery, Negro Cast, Political, Prison, Public Service, War, Western. . . . Edward could never make his imagination run down the rails of established formula. But with a family to support, he kept trying.

After 5:30 Edward had the good sense to take Anne to events other than boxing matches once in a while, events such as Hollywood's frequent and showy movie premieres. Edward was, as always, intensely interested in the technique of the motion picture, while Anne was on the lookout for famous faces. Anne discovered Marlene Dietrich in one crowd and audibly said that Dietrich was the skinniest woman she had ever seen. On another occasion, Anne spotted a marcelled Joan Bennett, whose appearance pleased Edward more; she did not have the slim, lean look that many film actresses strove for. Once Anne saw a stylish woman in a black sheath who looked like Gloria Swan-

James, a boxer, and Edward

son, and dressed like Swanson, and walked like Swanson. But Anne could not be sure, and Edward would chuckle inwardly at her uncertainty.

Every week, however, with Anne in tow, Edward went to the professional boxing matches in Los Angeles. The fights attracted a good many fans from the movie colony. The Andersons almost always sat directly behind Mae West and her silver-haired manager. The most famous passion goddess of the era, the performer who claimed to have introduced shimmy dancing to New York in 1919, the author of naughty plays with such names as *Sex* and *Diamond Lil,* Mae West surprised the Andersons with her relative petiteness. Like Anne herself, Miss West stood 5'5" and weighed 120 pounds, although she managed to seem slightly taller by piling high her platinum blonde hair. Ironically, the actress's father, John Patrick West, had been a prize-fighter early in life (which perhaps accounts for her interest in pugilism) before drifting into a career as a private detective. Mae West, who earned $300,000 per picture at her peak in the thirties, with an additional $100,000 for writing the story, was at that time about to make her last big success with Universal, playing Flora Belle Lee to W. C. Fields's Cuthbert J. Twillie in *My Little Chickadee,* which was released in 1940. After completing the film, she would praise Fields as "a great performer," but, herself a teetotaler, West would admit that "my only doubts about him came in bottles." Anne Anderson might have said something similar about Edward, who seemed to be drinking more as the thirties faded.

The kids were growing like vacant-lot weeds. When Edward and Anne moved into the white stucco bungalow with hardwood floors at Burbank, Helen looked around with delight at the wide and wonderful streets, lined with Spanish stucco houses and many trees and flowers. She was now between four and five years old and capable of enjoying some of the more worldly delights of the Los Angeles area. She liked ice cream — the Big Bear coconut ice-cream bars that mother brought home — but best of all she liked to go into the Hollywood ice-cream shop that was shaped like an inverted ice-cream cone. California merchants, taking their cue from motion-picture sets, dramatized their goods by building orange-drink stands shaped like oranges and motel units shaped like tepees.

Grandma Pearl — Helen called her "Pel" — decided she wanted to work and in 1939 got a Social Security card and a job as a seamstress with

Dick Edward and Helen

a Hollywood firm that put together period costumes for motion pictures. Through Helen's eyes, Pel worked in a marvelous shop with a high stairway in back, up which a preschooler, with considerable exertion, could mount to an interior balcony at the rear of the building. What's more, the shop had box upon box of antique buttons, all kinds, very beautiful and fascinating to a little girl.

For a child it was wonderland, and she would remember it with an overwhelming nostalgia a half century later. She liked the Burbank house; she liked the surrounding hills with flowers on their slopes. She felt her parents were happy. She could not know that her mother was worried about her father's increased drinking, hardly a thing a mother would discuss in the nursery.

Edward Anderson's increased elbow-bending was inconspicuous in the hard-drinking Hollywood crowd. His manner did not fit the egocentric Hollywood stereotype, typically brash, even loudmouthed. Yet he looked right. Gone were the days of the red vest, black derby, and umbrella that Anderson had when he left Ardmore, Oklahoma. He went to work in the writers' building at Warners in slacks, open-throated shirt, and sport coat. No hat. The ladies found Anderson handsome all his life, and he in turn would be able to admire on the lot or in the Greenroom such Warners leading ladies as Mary Astor, Joan Blondell, Ruth Chatterton, Joan Crawford, Bette Davis, Olivia de Havilland, Kay Francis, Ruby Keeler, Ann Sheridan, Marie Wilson, Jane Wyman, Loretta Young, and a hundred starlets, stand-ins, and Warners secretaries. Edward, however, remained devoted to Anne and their two children. His principal foible remained his continuing search for the inspiration that his pal John Knox had said he found at the bottom of a whiskey glass.

While he drank Anderson also read. He read when he got up in the morning, at the lunch table, after working hours. And as with drinking, Anderson now preferred his literature hundred proof, even in magazines — *Esquire* and *Story* and the like. He read and reread Knut Hamsun; his Hamsun volumes had accompanied him to Louisiana, Texas, Colorado, California, wherever he went.

Anderson soon discovered Stanley Rose's famous Hollywood bookstore. The thirty-eight-year-old Rose was said to do 5 percent of his business with motion picture companies and 90 percent with individuals connected with the movies. A competitor, Louis Epstein of the Pickwick Bookshop, said that Rose was legendary in the 1930s. "The doors of all the motion picture studios were open to him at all times, and . . . his studio visits often would start a book off to best-sellerdom," Epstein said.

Edward and Stanley were soon on first-name terms, and Anderson often began his visits by going back for a chat in the bookseller's office, a room whose walls were covered with photographs of Hollywood's most famous residents, including a trigger-quick shot of Carmen Miranda, her skirt swirling, her lack of underwear obvious.

Anne liked to go along on the visits to Stanley Rose's, but not into the office where the awful picture hung. She instead browsed through the shelves of books. On occasion she ran into living, breathing movie stars there. Once a 6'3" 195-pound browser with a familiar face came along. He asked her what book she was leafing through. Shyly, Anne told him. Then it came to her. The face belonged to Anthony Quinn, who had played a Valentino-like role in the recent film *Last Train from Madrid.*

Unlike some actors, Quinn was at home among books. He had

even written a drama himself, *Thirty-three Men,* which he had sold to a Broadway producer in 1937, the same year he married Katherine DeMille, the adopted daughter of Cecil B. DeMille.

Quinn, amused by the way this attractive woman was trying not to stare at him, said something else trivial. She replied, smiled. He asked, "Do I look like a Mexican to you?" The actor's father was Frank Quinn, an Irishman, and his mother was Manuella (Oaxaca) Quinn, a Mexican woman of Aztec descent. Anthony Quinn had been born in 1916 in Chihuahua, but during the Pancho Villa revolution his parents had brought him to El Paso, and when he was four, to Los Angeles, where his father became a cameraman at Selig Studio. Little Anthony had played a juvenile Tarzan in a jungle film before his father died in a car accident in 1925. Like Anderson, Quinn had not gone on to college but had tried his hand at sculpting, playing the saxophone in an orchestra, and preaching in Aimee Semple McPherson's temple. He had worked as a cement mixer, ditchdigger, boxer, fruit picker, taxi driver, and foreman in a mattress factory. After joining the Federal Theater Project, Quinn got his first big break in a part for Mae West's play, *Clean Beds,* in 1936.

"Do you know that I'm a Mexican?" the towering actor persisted. He would not become an American citizen until 1947.

Quinn had moved on by the time Edward came out of Rose's office. Anne told him about Quinn. Edward grinned for her; actors never meant much to him, and they meant even less after a year in Hollywood. He would have been more interested if he had known of Quinn's boxing days, or his admiration for such writers as Saroyan and Thomas Wolfe.

Edward and Anne did not realize that Stanley Rose was on the verge of closing his bookshop, that 1939 would be that institution's final year. Too many actors whose stars had faded owed him money; too many rising directors and screenwriters were too busy to pay their bookstore bills. Rose would soon engineer the sale of Saroyan's *Human Comedy,* tucking away a commission of ten thousand dollars on the deal, and become a literary agent, handling the work of Dick O'Conner, Louis Stevens, Theodore Bonnet, Audie Murphy, Pat McCormick, and many others.

Anderson's work at Warner Brothers brought him into contact with Edward G. Robinson, who invited the Andersons to his home for a party. Anne would have mixed feelings as she put on her best bib and tucker for the occasion, and Edward would be quietly amused at her apprehensions concerning a visit to this man whom she had seen on the screen as a beetle-faced archvillain with fiercely furrowed brows and wide mouth stretched in angry snarls or cruel smiles.

After spending 1912 and 1913 studying at the American Academy of Dramatic Arts, Robinson worked his way up to stardom on the New York stage during the twenties in such varied roles as the effeminate emperor in the Theater Guild's 1925 production of Shaw's *Androcles and the Lion,* as General Díaz for the 1926 production of *Juárez and Maximilian,* and as the epileptic brother in *The Brothers Karamazov* during 1927. In Hollywood, however, Robinson had achieved his first film success as the gangster in Warners' *Little Caesar* in 1931, and under the stock company system then used on the West Coast this versatile actor was offered only roles as hard-boiled types, generally gangsters, in the ensuing years. He would not land the role of a decent, emotionally normal man until *Dr. Erlich's Magic Bullet,* which was released in 1940.

The Andersons drove out to the house on Edward and Gladys Robinson's little farm in the hills and canyons above Beverly Hills. The Robinsons were living there while Sam Marx remodeled their Beverly Hills house, and they also hoped their six-year-old son, Manny, would profit from the "rural" life there. Edward G. Robinson at this time was also worried by the rise of Hitler and the impending horrors he feared would sweep Europe. Despite his forty-six years, Robinson even briefly considered trying to join the French Army. The actor let none of this show at the party; he was a delightful host.

A smiling Robinson, without a jacket or tie, welcomed the Andersons as he did the other guests. Inside, the actor, steadily freshened drinks and nudged the conversation just enough to keep it moving along casually, pleasantly. He was solicitous of everyone's comfort.

Robinson and Anne discovered a mutual liking for parades, for garish floats and brassy music and clowns; they discussed them at some length. Even Anne's shy husband relaxed in such an atmosphere, talked a little more, and wore a natural smile. When, years later, the Andersons learned of Robinson's distinguished collection of Impressionist and Post-Impressionist paintings, they would wonder where it had been in the days they knew him. The fact was that Robinson had put it on loan to the Los Angeles Museum for the two and a half years their home was being remodeled. Sam Marx, an art collector himself, changed their home so radically as to practically rebuild it, making the entire lower part of the house a gallery for Robinson's collection.

Meanwhile, Anderson had turned his football screenplay, *An American Hero,* into a novel. It was a little shorter than the average novel, but hadn't Thornton Wilder gotten away with that on his *Bridge of San Luis Rey,* which came out in 1927? Anderson's agent went the rounds with *American Hero* in New York, but no publisher fell in love with it. He decided to send it to his agent across the Atlantic, A. M. Heath and Company, to try the London publishers.

California towns, far off from the rest of America, seem on the road to nowhere. The bordering Pacific is too vast and empty; the southwestern deserts isolate California from the Midwest and East. In the early thirties, Edmund Wilson called one California port city "the jumping-off place." Still, visitors from Edward's past turned up from time to time on the Anderson doorstep. One day Edward answered a knock and opened the door to see the familiar figure of the pastor of Abilene's First Presbyterian Church, the Reverend Dr. T. S. Knox, who was visiting California on church business. Although Edward during this era spared little time for Christian ministers, he had time for this one. Dr. Knox could talk with him about many things of interest, about Abilene happenings, about the Hollywood milieu, about literary matters. It was some time before Dr. Knox got his hat and disappeared from their lives, for the last time.

Anderson had fallen into step with the other writers at the studios, drink for drink. And writers of that era, beginning daily about breakfast time, applied themselves seriously to alcohol. Of the first six American winners of the Nobel Prize for literature—all of whom were active in the thirties—half were alcoholics: Sinclair Lewis, who won in 1930; Eugene O'Neill, 1936; William Faulkner, 1949. Of the other half, Ernest Hemingway, 1954, and John Steinbeck, 1962, were hard drinkers. Many of their un-awarded contemporaries were just as dedicated to booze.

Naturally enough, Anderson tended to fall in with the writers who were ex-newspapermen, and that crowd were notably heavy drinkers even in that boozing generation. The best known among these was Gene Fowler. Anne, whose Methodist background never quite allowed her to approve of all this imbibing, got a good look at Fowler when Edward took her to a party at Fowler's place. Gene was a big man, a good four inches taller than Edward, with graying red hair. He was almost fifty, fifteen years older than Edward. Despite his success, Fowler spurned the affluent image, continuing to wear cheap suits and palling around with other newspapermen-turned-screenwriters, such as Ben Hecht, Charles MacArthur, and the like, several of whom Anderson met through him.

Aside from their long careers in journalism, Anderson and Fowler had other things in common. Anderson had come to Hollywood from Denver; Fowler had grown up in Denver and had landed his first reporting job on a Denver newspaper (Fowler's nickname was "Pride of the Rockies"). Anderson was fascinated by boxing; Fowler had managed several pugilists and wrestlers. Anderson had served as press agent for Texas politician William McCraw; Fowler had acted as press agent for Queen Marie of Rumania. Both men were novelists; Fowler published *Illusion in Java* about that time. Both were drawn to Hollywood's big, steady money; Fowler would later say that *Illusion in Java* had cost him $25,000 for travel, plus $90,000 in screenplay writing that he had to decline, while his royalties from the novel amounted to a comparatively slim four thousand dollars; Anderson's book royalties had hardly put him on easy street. Both wrote in a frank and realistic manner: Anderson's novels were locked up "in jail" by Maude Cole at Abilene Public Library; Fowler's play *The Great Magoo* was called "college boy wash-room stuff" by critic George Jean Nathan.

It's a pity that Anderson never saw fit to write a novel about Hollywood. His steady, hard-to-hoodwink prose possessed a flat reportorial quality that would have opened a window on a film capital entirely different from the intellectual window of Aldous Huxley's *After Many a Summer Dies the Swan,* or the fiercely satiric window of Evelyn Waugh's *The Loved One,* or the low view of high life in Budd Schulberg's *What Makes Sammy Run?* He might have chosen to examine the view of the movie-making army's buck privates and camp followers found in Nathanael West's *The Day of the Locust,* but Anderson would have shaped the material in a manner a world apart from West's surrealism.

He did write on other subjects during this time. Along with steady daily drinking, Edward would launch a really big toot every time a manuscript came back with a rejection note attached to it. Bernice Baumgartern, who still represented Anderson for Brandt and Brandt, was unable to get a U.S. publisher interested in his *Seven Hundred Wives,* which sent him off on a round of bars.

Because he much admired Arnold Gingrich's new magazine, *Es-*

quire, Anderson tailored a new essay, "Why Men Get Drunk as the Lord," especially for it. *Esquire* declined. Edward got drunk as the lord. Other magazine stories and nonfiction pieces were also near misses, and provided Edward with other excuses for drowning his sorrows.

Edward's novelization of *An American Hero* also returned unsuccessful from its tour of English publishing houses. Anderson's first two novels had been published in England by the firm of William Heinemann, Limited. That firm's director, A. Dwye Evans, wrote Anderson in 1938 that:

> . . . we have decided that it would be in the interests of us both if we were to wait and publish your next full length novel. Your reputation in this country has been growing steadily and *Thieves Like Us,* as you know, received very favorable opinions indeed from the critics — particularly James Agate, who carries a certain amount of weight here. I feel with a book as short as this and with a subject matter of little interest to the English, that it would be a mistake to jeopardise this growing reputation. . . .

James Agate's literary esteem did little to pay for groceries. Finally, on March 29, 1939, Edward sold Roland Brown the film rights to *Thieves Like Us* for a skimpy five hundred dollars. Anne was more than a little annoyed when her husband came home and told her about it. Brown would hold the rights for a little over two years before selling them to RKO for ten thousand dollars.

13. Barrymore's Passing

Edward E. Anderson was sitting in the corridor of Hollywood Presbyterian Hospital during May of 1942, sitting there in that ramrod-straight posture of a short man who knows in the depths of his subconscious that he must not slump like taller men. He was one of a group of men, most of them journalists, who smoked and talked in low tones, but whose underlying attention was focused on the door of one nearby room. They were waiting for John Barrymore, who occupied the room, to die.

In the first part of the twentieth century, John Barrymore was one of the most famous actors in America, and also one of the best. (In the fickle world of the theater the two do not necessarily go hand in hand.) His portrayal of Hamlet had won him international renown. John had been born in 1882; his father was a celebrated actor, Maurice Barrymore, who had taken that stage name after growing up as Herbert Blythe. His mother was Georgiana Drew Barrymore; the Drews were already a famous theatrical family. Like his older brother Lionel, John had tried to escape the stage by becoming a painter, but the charming, fun-loving John inevitably returned to the theatre, playing his roles brilliantly. His role as a husband was less well played; he went through four unsuccessful marriages, drank heavily, and earned huge amounts on stage, screen, and radio, but spent it all, and more.

Barrymore's career was at the same time illustrious and ill-regulated. Anderson, sitting in the hospital corridor, looking at the smoke rising from his cigarette, had time to ponder Barrymore's past. And his own.

When Anderson's job at Warners ran out, economic necessity forced him to return to the newspapering work he loathed. Leaving Burbank, Edward had managed to catch on with the little newspaper at Santa

Barbara, a town of thirty-five thousand that was ninety-four miles up the coast from Los Angeles.

Helen Ann was five and Dick Edward three, both full of high spirits. When Anderson kept them, he sometimes let them take off all their clothes and run with a kind of wild, pagan joy from one end of the house to the other. At that age the children were not self-conscious, nor would they notice that daddy drank more now, or that now mama occasionally argued with him, no longer letting him make every decision uncontested.

While Anderson was holding down his newspaper job and in his off hours trying to get a book started, he often put aside a few minutes at the children's bedtime to smooth the road to sleep. In the nursery he would play his harmonica and sing:

Come and sit by my side, little darling;
Do not hasten to bid me adieu,
But remember the Red River Valley,
And the one who has loved you so true.

He preferred sad songs—"Am I Blue," "If I Had the Wings of an Angel."

Helen Ann was her father's favorite. He made no excuses for having a favorite and believed it natural for a father to prefer a daughter. (The intelligentsia of the thirties had found a prophet in Dr. Freud.)

Anne had grown up in America without ever possessing a bicycle, so Edward now bought her a bike. Some mornings he borrowed it to pump little Helen Ann on a thrilling ride to her Santa Barbara kindergarten.

When the forties began, the Andersons moved to a place in Topanga Canyon off the Roosevelt Highway, roughly thirty miles west of Los Angeles. In the canyon the Andersons lived in a house of knotty pine with a big front porch. The rear of the house was jammed against a mountain, and most of the living space was upstairs. There was a garage downstairs. Helen Ann thought it was a wonderful house. The Andersons were among two thousand persons whose homes were scattered along the nine miles of Topanga Canyon, which runs from the Santa Monica Mountains southward to the sea. California holly grew on the slopes of the canyon. Thickets of sycamores and alders grew in the lower part of the canyon bordering Topanga Creek. Beneath the surface of the land, laid down when the area was the floor of the sea, lay buried the roots and branches of a Miocene forest.

Edward, who was working now at the *Los Angeles Examiner*, commuted in their gray Buick, and he did not arrive home until two o'clock in the morning. Edward liked the location, but he did not like driving a car, ever. Anne did not like the lonely house, altogether too far from neighbors to suit her, waiting for Edward in the dark, still nights. When he finally would arrive, he generally had news ink on his hands. She quizzed him about printing, and he made a stab at explaining points and picas, column widths and type sizes.

He continued to work seriously at writing. Little Helen was impressed to see her father get a pencil and pad, move to a comfortable chair over by a window, and write. But all too often he drank, and that tended to darken Anne's perennial optimism.

The family went on frequent picnics. Anne would drive, stopping at a neighborhood grocery first to buy goose liver, crackers, and other makings. On one such trip, when Edward had been drinking, the family car was halted at a railway crossing while a freight train passed slowly in front of it. Telling Anne and the kids that he would show them how to hop a train, Edward got out, jogged a moment beside the track, and swung himself up into an empty boxcar that passed. It frightened the children. It frightened Anne, because for a brief second she thought he was taking to the road again. But as the train gathered speed Edward swung off again less than a hundred yards down the track. He walked back to the car so they could continue on their way to the picnic. Often the family drove along the winding road to Topanga Beach or other picnic sites singing:

Yo ho ho, you and me,
Little brown jug, how I love thee!

But on that day it was a while before anyone struck up a song again.

There were varmints around the Topanga house. On one occasion, a large snake came writhing through the area where the children were playing. Edward courageously went out and killed it, which made him something of a hero to little Helen and Dick Edward. Then Jim, the caretaker, strolled by. "My God, Anderson, you've killed a king snake! That's a five-hundred-dollar fine, because they're the only thing that kills rattlers. We'd better get to digging." A somewhat crestfallen hero, Edward hastily dug a hole to bury the snake.

In the fateful year of 1941, with the United States teetering on the edge of the spreading world conflict, the Andersons moved again, establishing themselves at 1228 South New Hampshire in Los Angeles. The house they rented was an old, white frame house, built around 1900, with six vast rooms, and bay windows. Anne, who was now expecting their third child, liked it better because its location was not as frighteningly lonely to her as the Topanga Canyon house.

Since Edward still did not exchange letters, he was hardly aware that back in Abilene his mother had moved to 1929 North Third Street, where the family got by on what E. H. had left, added to the money earned by Dorothy as a clerk at the Farmers and Merchants National Bank and by Louise as a beauty operator at Rene Beauty Service. Edward's librarian friend, Maude E. Cole, was nearing retirement at sixty-two and that year saw her only novel, *Wind against Stone,* published by Lyman House of Los Angeles.

Edward continued to battle booze. But he developed an even more sinister passion than his love of drink; he became anti-Semitic. The fascism of Hitler and Mussolini had certain intellectual claims that interested Anderson, but more important, however, was the influence of Anderson's idol, Knut Hamsun. In World War I Hamsun had openly supported the German cause and in 1940 gave his public blessing to the Nazi invasion of Norway. Edward read Nazi arguments with approval. He even took Anne to a rally of American Nazis.

In one sense Anderson remained forever a provincial: He always took up fashions too late. His hobo novel came out after the vogue in proletarian novels was well past its peak; his bandit novel came out three years after John Dillinger and Clyde Barrow were safely dead and buried. If Edward had admired one of the totalitarian ideologies in the twenties or early thirties, his remarks would have been lost among the hurrahs of Lincoln Steffens, Booth Tarkington, John Reed, Ezra Pound, Robinson Jeffers, and many others — even, of all publications, Henry Luce's *Fortune* magazine. By the forties, however, almost everybody, including Neville Chamberlain, had grasped the wrongheadedness of dictatorships of the left or right.

In the South New Hampshire Street house was a black, upright piano. Edward would sit on the stool and pick out "Chopsticks," or Anne would play one of Edward's favorites, "Be Nobody's Darling But Mine."

The house had a big, fenced backyard, with several fig trees growing in it, a grand and glorious place for the children to play. Once they made hula skirts out of crepe paper and played at being islanders. On another occasion they played wild west with Dick Edward togged out as the Lone Ranger, a masked hero on the airwaves, and Helen as a pioneer woman.

As Anne's pregnancy approached its ninth month, Edward pitched in to take care of the kids. To simplify matters, he took scissors and cut their hair short so it wouldn't be necessary to brush it.

Grandma Pel pitched in to help, too. She taught Helen to sing popular songs such as "Won't You Come Over to My House," "Playmate," and "How I Love to Ride the Ferry," which little Helen sometimes chirped out for visitors. Pel also taught her granddaughter to recite Riley's "Little Orphan Annie."

Everybody in the family savored music, but the vocal talent was unevenly distributed, as anyone might admit after listening to Edward singing a frequently off-key "In the Shade of the Old Apple Tree" or "Let the Rest of the World Go By." Dick Edward, like his dad, enjoyed music but couldn't carry a tune in a sack.

Edward and Anne's third child, a boy, was born November 7, 1941. Since this was only a month before the United States was catapulted into World War II by the Japanese attack on the American fleet in Hawaii, Edward's suggestion that the child be named Raeder for a prominent officer in the German navy wasn't exactly in harmony with American sentiment. Anne softened this by adding "Ross." The child had a troubled beginning: measles at three months, chicken pox at five months, whooping cough at seven months.

Pel often took the two older children to Clifton's Cafeteria, another fantasyland-inspired "theme" institution. You entered through a fake cave passageway, and inside there were precious stones in the wall, a waterfall, and palm trees. Given a coin, little Helen would insert it in a slot and a dish of ice cream would come sliding down a hill of stage-prop volcanic rock.

Edward's sympathy with the fascists and his anti-Semitism were more abstract than practical. After all, he got on well with his Jewish employer Ben Schulberg, secretary Sydelle Tarshis, agent Bernice Baumgartern, and with various newspaper colleagues who were Jewish. When war was declared, he had no intention of betraying his country. He wore a Civil Defense armband for duties during those early days of the war when no one knew whether a Japanese fleet might appear at any moment on the West Coast.

John Barrymore had collapsed May 19, 1942, at a broadcast studio where he had gone to do his much-needed rehearsing for his weekly radio show. Since the mid-thirties Barrymore's memory had increasingly failed him, a failing particularly serious for an actor, who needs to remember lines. Cue cards, radio scripts, and witty improvisation enabled him to continue, in one way or another, earning money from his craft. But at age sixty he had simply burned out his physical resources. Even back in 1936, the year in which Anderson had gone to Kerrville to write *Thieves Like Us,* Barrymore's physical tolerance for alcohol had worn so thin that a few ounces of the stuff would intoxicate him. Dr. Hugo Kersten, who attended the actor toward the end of his life, estimated that Barrymore had drunk 640 barrels of booze since the turn of the century. Now in 1942 Barrymore's basic ailment was cirrhosis of the liver, but he was also suffering from kidney failure, chronic gastritis, ulceration of the esophagus, hardening of the arteries, chronic eczema, and pneumonia.

In a room near John Barrymore's hospital room, his older brother Lionel waited. He would occasionally chat with Anderson and other members of the fourth estate. In many ways Lionel was the most variously gifted of his famous family. Like John, he was a draftsman and a painter. When the movies found their voice at the end of the twenties, Lionel, because of his experience in the legitimate theater, was asked to direct several films. He complied innovatively, directing such films as *His Glorious Night, The Rogue Song,* and *Ten Cents a Dance.* Lionel also composed music, which was played by the New York Philharmonic and other symphony orchestras, and toward the end of his life he would write novels and other books. Waiting for his brother's death, Lionel struggled with his own burden of pain: inflammatory rheumatism, arthritis, and a twice-broken left hip that never healed properly. He would be confined to a wheelchair the rest of his long and distinguished career, but at that time Metro-Goldwyn-Mayer was worried that his crippling ailments would hurt his star image; Anderson and the others agreed to keep Lionel Barrymore's ailments out of their stories on John's final illness.

When John Barrymore's body and mind had begun to wear out with hard, careless usage, his friends had rallied to him. They had called themselves the "Barrymore Rescue Mission," and their ranks included Gene Fowler, John Decker, Alan Dinehart, Alan Mowbray, Thomas Mitchell — even W. C. Fields. Now those who happened to be in town could only visit his hospital room; rescue was no longer possible.

Anderson and the other newspapermen at the dying actor's door watched Barrymore's friends come and go. Anderson knew Gene Fowler and John Decker fairly well, and they were particularly faithful, often keeping vigil in the room across the hall. The vigil ended shortly after ten o'clock on Friday, May 29, 1942.

Anderson's interest in John Barrymore went a good deal deeper than that of most reporters who were with him on the death watch. Anderson had thought seriously of writing a book on the scamp of the Barrymore clan. When *Seven Hundred Wives* failed to generate real interest, and the novelized *An American Hero* was flatly turned down by publishers, Anderson had looked around for a solid nonfiction project. John Barrymore's heroic drinking, love affairs, marriages, and high-spirited eccentricities were legendary in Hollywood. *The Royal Family,* a hit play by George S. Kaufman and Edna Ferber that obviously depicted the Barrymore family under the name "Cavendish," was made into a motion picture in 1930, and John's quixotic character became known to the entire nation. Anderson, quite rightly, felt that a biography of John would sell. If show-business biographies tend to have a shorter life in print than books dealing with statesmen and generals, show-business books nevertheless often produce large, quick profits.

With his usual thoroughness, Anderson had begun reading up on Barrymore. Close at hand were Barrymore's friends and associates. At a party at the home of Gene Fowler, Anderson mentioned Barrymore. Fowler had been a drinking buddy of Barrymore's since 1918, when the drama editor of the *New York American* sent Fowler out to interview the actor, then starring in a successful run of Tolstoy's *Redemption.* Fowler was fifteen years older than Anderson, but their common newspaper background made them at ease with one another.

Then Edward and Anne had dinner with artist John Decker. (Gossip had it that Decker had painted a mural at Barrymore's home depicting a variety of erotic activities.) Decker listened to Anderson's proposal for writing a book, but the artist was not encouraging. "You'd have to know the man personally to write it," Decker told Anderson. "You couldn't possibly write it without having known the man."

Other research attempts also bogged down or fizzled out, and Anderson finally abandoned the project. Fowler himself would eventually write the Barrymore biography, *Good Night, Sweet Prince,* and his many personal anecdotes about his friend undoubtedly added to the interest of the book. It was published in 1944, sold 105,000 copies in its first three weeks, and remained on the best-seller list the rest of the year.

In the biography, Fowler specifically denies that he had been following his friend John Barrymore around and keeping Boswell-like notes on his bons mots, preparing to write Barrymore's biography. Only after the actor died, and friends such as Ashton Stevens and Richard Watts, Jr., began to advise him on the project, did Fowler feel impelled to write the biography.

If Anderson had persisted and actually written a Barrymore biography, his matter-of-fact prose would have produced a book quite different from the one Fowler wrote in the frilly prose typical of newspapers in the fin-de-siecle era.

14. Sacramento

Over in the *Examiner* newsroom, Edward Anderson made one too many wisecracks about the international Jewish conspiracy. He was fired.

Giving up at least temporarily his hopes of building a nest in the motion-picture industry, Edward wrote the woman who ran the *Sacramento Bee*. She gladly gave him a job. Seven months after the Pearl Harbor attack, the wartime military draft was making it difficult to find good newspaper hands. Thirty-seven years old, married, father of three, Edward was relatively draft-proof. Sacramento could hardly compare with Los Angeles, but still it was the capital of California, with a population of almost 100,000 and with lots going on.

Anne was not slow to tell Edward that she didn't like the house they rented outside Sacramento in July of 1942. The frame shotgun house seemed haunted by the sad echoes of its former Japanese occupants, who had been sent away to an internment camp. Edward liked the remoteness of the place, its back-to-the-land quality. In this he showed his usual knack for taking up an intellectual movement after it had crested; in the thirties back-to-the-land movements, led by William Barsodi, M. G. Kains, and others, had been in vogue.

The Anderson children, at least Helen and Dick Edward, who were old enough to get out and around, had still another viewpoint. They liked the Japanese house, with its washing machine on the back porch and its mysterious old car they could peep at inside the garage. They also peeped through the windows and cracks of the old barn, where they could see a children's tea set and many stored household goods of the Japanese family.

A Mexican-American family was their closest neighbor. The mother kept burlap bags full of tortillas. Anne lent orange juice to her; the neighbor woman believed that it helped her baby to walk, an idea Anne laughed about when she told Edward. One day a neighbor kid threw a rock at Helen. Edward argued about it with the neighbor father, knocking him down in the process.

Anne told Helen that daddy and the other man were both drinking. Helen saw that her mama and daddy argued more now, and she heard the mean things they said to each other.

Anne found the Japanese house as lonely as the place in Topanga Canyon, and she soon talked Edward into moving to another house, closer in, on West Davis Road. Although it was at the extreme edge of town, neighbors were scattered along the highway, including, hard by, a bar and grocery whose owner kept a great Saint Bernard dog. The bar was handy, in fact too handy, for a man of Edward's increasing thirst. Anne tried to make the best of things and planted a victory garden.

Still they went on picnics. One day Edward was acting sillier than usual and drove the car right up to the edge of the river, which made Helen squeal with fright. On another picnic they saw a man drown; a man who was wading on the other side of the river stepped into a deep hole and just disappeared, as quickly and as completely as a soap bubble from Dick Edward's bubble pipe. Another day the family was riding home on a bus when sirens began to scream. Edward, Anne, and the children got off the bus and went to the scene of a shooting, where they saw the body of a deputy sheriff murdered with a shotgun when he tried to serve a warrant. Next day the children heard Edward tell Anne that four officers had cornered the murderer in a fenced yard, cornered him and put eleven bullets in him.

Less exciting events were fun, too. One day Edward and Anne and another couple brought some Chinese food home to West Davis Road, and the children got their first taste of chop suey. Later Anne watched Helen learn to ride the bicycle Edward had bought Anne. Dick Edward was green with envy. The youngest was big enough now to play with toy soldiers, and he watched the real soldiers in long truck convoys passing the house.

Edward had gone to Sacramento with the idea of hacking out headlines and other newspaper "trash," as he considered it, for eight hours daily, and then, somehow, by a superhuman effort, writing quality magazine pieces as well as a serious book in his spare time. But newspaper work frequently drains a writer of the urge to write, an urge necessary to push through a big project such as a book. The typical hardcover work of a journalist is a collage of old columns or think-pieces, a rag quilt of intellectual patches with each patch containing roughly the same number of ideas as, say, a Victorian lyric poem. Anderson never got the knack for squeezing out such small creative nuggets, or wasn't born with it, or however you get it, as his signed newspaper columns later in life would show.

Finally he wised up; he couldn't do it. Anne, who once researched his true detective stories, had grown up in the tradition of the house-wife and nurturing mother, but she went out and got a job. Edward could then leave the newsroom to write seriously, full time.

Edward could have looked around himself on the West Davis highway and found plenty of characters to people a novel. Next door were Frenchy and Dorothy Goss, a friendly couple with a teenage son and daughter. Frenchy had lost a leg, and he kept a hundred dollars hidden inside his spare wooden leg, which stood casually in the corner of their bedroom. In the big auto-repair shop he owned, Frenchy got around with the aid of a single crutch. Dorothy Goss worked for the state and it was she who helped Anne also get a state job. In off hours, Frenchy played guitar with his own musical group at the Red Barn; Anne and Edward went dancing there.

On the other side lived a couple who operated the bar, grocery, and service station. They owned the house that the Andersons had rented. Their big Saint Bernard dog radiated beneficent protection around the place. Anne, her starchy Methodist upbringing showing, rather disapproved of the family putting their beautiful daughter Yolanda to tend the bar. Worse yet, it was just a few steps for Edward to go and toss down a drink. He discovered that he liked wine, and he liked it often.

A bit farther down was the place of a big German named Al Peel and his wife Mary. They sold diesel fuel. Al, who was about sixty years old, had walked from the East Coast all the way to California, with a pack on his back. Once he got his feet planted firmly in California, he sent for his wife, who was fifteen years his senior.

Aside from neighbors, the Andersons' friends included a hard-drinking couple they met through Edward's work at the *Bee*. The wife, quite drunk one night, insisted on driving Anne back to the West Davis highway. Edward and the husband, also drinking, had lingered at the

Andersons' when their wives originally left. Anne tried to remain calm during the wild return trip but had to reach over to help the drunk steer across a bridge; the side of the car scraped the bridge balusters, but Anne prevented a smash-up. The woman was laughing hysterically when they pulled up in front of the Anderson house. That laugh would echo down through four decades in Helen's memory.

During the Sacramento years, Anderson worked for a time on a novel about the West. He called it *Mighty Men of Valor,* a title he took from the sixth chapter of Judges. His experience with the radio show in Denver had provided him with some material and had led him to believe that he could write fiction about the frontier. Then a friend, Nivan Busch of RKO, got interested in Anderson's outline of a western set at Fort Griffin, a name Anderson took from a nineteenth-century frontier fort established near present-day Abilene by the U.S. Army to ward off the fierce Comanche raids. But nothing came of the novel. He wrote a short story about Sam Houston, and another about a brutal, narrow early settler who mistreated his family. Neither sold.

The thirties were over, and Anderson couldn't seem to find the literary key to the forties, but he continued to search the bottom of the whiskey glass for inspiration. He seldom bothered to mail a once-rejected manuscript out to a second market, going on his customary drinking bender instead. With writing and rejections and bills and the blues, the novelist found excuses to stay sozzled most of the time.

Anne's job was no government sinecure; she worked at cutting state employment checks, at operating sorting and collating machinery. She came home evenings weary from work, and she was increasingly alarmed at the idleness of her husband, at his frequent visits to the bar next door. Wine and love were growing sour.

Eventually Anne came home to a development that was too much. One of the children ran to meet her. His clothes were muddy and wet. What had happened? The child managed to get across that he had fallen into a nearby irrigation ditch, and since nobody was around to help him out, he had through heroic effort climbed out by himself. It was the last straw. Anne stormed into the house. There, stretched across the bed, obviously in an alcoholic stupor, lay her husband. Nearby on a table stood his typewriter, and in it a sheet of paper—totally blank.

Anne, who had been so in awe of her husband that she could not openly oppose his sending the children away when they came to California, let her pent-up frustration spew forth in a speech made eloquent by her boiling anger. Edward sat up, then stood up, not so much a sobered man now as a wide-awake drunk. She asked him a pivotal question.

"Why did you marry me anyway?"

"Because you were the only damned virgin I could find."

"Well, isn't that romantic!"

He slapped her.

She rushed forward, and they wrestled, tumbling to the floor, a bitter parody of the embrace of lovers. Edward, in spite of his drunken state, was much the more powerful of the two; as they rolled over and over, he began to pin her arms. Anne, in the violence of her anger, found only one way to assert herself.

She bit a big chunk out of the top of his left ear.

So this tumbling of a child, this bitter perversion of a tender hug and ear-nip, this climactic explosion ripped the marriage apart. Edward gathered up a few clothes and moved into a rooming house in town. Dorothy Goss drove Anne to town to see a lawyer and he helped her file for divorce. In California there would be a period of legal separation before the final divorce.

Anne still not like the sour deal Edward had struck with Roland Brown for the film rights to *Thieves Like Us*. Only five hundred. The more she thought about it, the more furious she became. Her own part in that book welled up in her like ill-digested delicacies inside an ulcer sufferer: her struggles with the cranky stove in Kerrville, the hours interviewing Roy Johnson at Huntsville penitentiary, her brainstorming about exactly what Keechie would reply to Bowie.

Anne stormed into the office of her divorce attorney to demand what could be done. The attorney questioned her about the circumstances. Then he told her what she could do legally.

Nothing.

The separation of Anne and Edward proved uncomfortable for them both. Despite all their recent troubles, Edward and Anne had begun their marriage passionately in love, and their attraction for one another remained strong. Edward frequently left his Sacramento rooming house to visit Anne and the kids. He just hung around, obviously reluctant to let her go. She knew that things had gone bad for them, but her heart was glad when he turned up at the house. Before the divorce became final, they decided to patch things up. Anne considered it a new, second marriage.

Edward moved back in. Anne returned to work. Edward returned to drinking. The marriage contained an irreparable flaw, like a car with a busted block. Anne's sister and brother-in-law, Ruby and Jay B. Hendricks, had moved to Glendora, California, during the war. Now they were moving back to Abilene, and they took little Helen with them. Finally, Anne said, I'm going back to Texas too.

Edward understood that their second try at marriage had failed, but he allowed that he might just as well go back, too.

So they gave their Victoria-model Ford to their bartender-landlord as payment for the back rent they owed him. It didn't matter; they hadn't been able to drive it much. Edward had just showed up one day, out of the blue, you might say, driving this handsome black car with a red stripe around it. But he still didn't like to drive, and they couldn't get much gas because of wartime rationing.

Anne and Edward took the children down to the station to buy tickets on a train jammed with American servicemen. Aboard there was much noise — stirring about, talking, singing. Edward occasionally took a nip from some bottled goods he had stashed in the hand luggage; Anne bitterly remembered her victory garden vegetables, which she had canned herself and been forced to leave behind. The thirties were definitely over.

15. Domestic Changes

One day in the late 1940s Edward Anderson drove out of Fort Worth and headed down the 153-mile stretch of highway that led to Abilene. He hated to drive, but his ex-wife and his three children had an irresistible attraction for him.

He was sober.

He steered the late-model car, borrowed from his sister Imogene, past the wit of Burma Shave quatrains on fence posts, down the long highway through his birthplace of Weatherford, past the failed mining town of Thurber. The enormous chimney, thrusting skyward in front of the slag heaps of ruined Thurber, seemed a symbol of the two novels left behind in his own ruined career. As he steered toward Abilene, Edward was also trying to steer back to the high road of his own life, a road that, somewhere back around Los Angeles or Sacramento, he had detoured from.

Along the roadside the vegetation dried up into West Texas.

He could only feel ambivalent about Anne. In 1946, Anne had divorced Edward. The divorce became final, ironically, on Edward's birthday, June 19. After seeing him tumble through careers as novelist and screenwriter and back into the newspapering he loathed (he now had a job with the *Fort Worth Star-Telegram*) Anne had struck out on her own. She blamed his drinking.

Up he went, climbing Ranger Hill, the slope up which, within Edward's memory, Model-T drivers had backed in order to get a gear sufficient to make the grade.

Anne, so they said, was now working at some drugstore in Abilene. He had charmed a few females since they had parted; did she have a new man? The question would stab him, and require him again to fight off the desire for an anesthetizing drink. He drove on through Eastland, Cisco, Putnam, Baird, and Clyde, towns in which the tallest building was usually the courthouse.

Abilene was the first place west of Fort Worth to have a true skyline. Coming up the Bankhead Highway, three and a half miles east of Abilene, Edward caught sight, a little off to the right, of the clustered buildings of the business district: tallest of them the sixteen-story Wooten Hotel, from which his old pal Houston Heitchew had plunged; the shorter Hilton Hotel, the yellow-brick Mims Building, and the red-brick Alexander Building.

Over Lytle Creek Bridge. Past the Spanish Courts, the Landau Courts, and Abilene Courts, past Abilene Casket Company and Schlumberger Well Surveying, past greasy-spoon cafes and a Pentecostal church, Edward would turn north and drive across the railroad tracks, past the Carnegie Library, rich in memories, to pull up near the yellow-brick building, mostly doctors' offices, where Anne worked. His blood pressure climbed a little.

Now in her early thirties, missing the softness and shyness of a dozen years earlier, now slim, sophisticated, and lovely, Anne stood behind the pharmacy cash register. When she finished ringing up her customer, she turned to Edward.

It's you, is it.

How are things with you?

You can see for yourself.

He looked around: a cheesy place, not much of a drugstore by American standards, no soda fountain, no cosmetics or electric razors, no gifts or gegaws. The pharmacy was small and crammed almost entirely with medicines. Like Anne, it was lean and without frivolity.

What time do you get off?

She told him, and agreed that he could pick her up; Anne had begun softening toward Edward the minute he showed up in that little medical building pharmacy. Her reservations about their ability to live together, acquired in the long and painful early forties, were slowly lulled during Edward's increasingly regular visits.

One at a time, he would take his children back to Dallas with him, to visit with his mother and sisters. Edward got along best with Helen, in her early teens now and going to movies on her own, even having an occasional date, such as when the future writer Sam Pendergrast took her to an Abilene YMCA party. Edward had the most trouble with Dick Edward, who was already rebellious; Dick Edward went to Dallas once with his father and refused to go again.

Anne had worked first at Lucile Guin's child-care facility when she returned to Abilene at war's end. Mr. Guin worked at the post office, and Mrs. Guin took care of children at their home. Anne and her children had lived in an apartment there also, but they moved on when she went to work for the pharmacy that served the physicians in the medical building. Edward sent her seventy-five dollars a month to help out.

After the 1946 divorce, Edward had continued to drink heavily in Dallas. He had borrowed money from Leon and Imogene for a futile trip to New York, where he found no market for his writing. In a Texas bar he discovered that his drinking companion was an ex-serviceman, and Edward's old sympathies with the fascists bubbled to the surface. Anderson frankly told the other fellow that he had been soldiering for the wrong side. The American veteran saw red, and in the ensuing battle he beat up Edward badly, breaking his jaw, sending him to the hospital.

Now Edward was making a grim effort to straighten his life. Along with his *Star-Telegram* job, Edward was seriously at work on fiction again. Agent Charles Schnel had read the manuscript of *Mighty Men of Valor,* liked its "wonderful masculine sense of humor," and compared it to the work of Sherwood Anderson. He encouraged Edward to write "the oil story" that had been germinating in the writer's mind. He had agreed to try to sell the movie rights to *Hungry Men;* he and Edward would split the proceeds fifty-fifty.

Edward showed up at Anne's Abilene doorstep one summer day in 1949 with the news that for the first time in his life he had bought a house. For her. He proposed to take her there as his bride again.

Anne said yes.

Edward always felt a tie with Weatherford even though the family had taken him away when he was tiny. (Once, on a trip to New York, he even took the trouble to look up Weatherford's other novelist, Edwin Lanham, author of *Sailors Don't Care* and *Thunder in the Earth.* Lanham was living in a penthouse. They didn't get along well.) Now Edward and Anne, with one of their children chaperoning, stopped in Weatherford to retie the legal knot on August 16, 1949. County Judge Joe Dodson officiated. He noticed the child and asked who the parents were.

"Oh, we are!"

Dodson commented wryly that perhaps it was time for the wedding, and began the ceremony.

The dream house, alas, was no vine-covered cottage with roses blooming. Anne was less than delighted when she moved the kids into the little dwelling, where she found not a stick of furniture. The house was on Cannon Street in Fort Worth, only a block and a half from the railroad tracks and their heavy traffic. Helen, now fifteen, accepted it because she knew her daddy loved railroads, but her mama didn't see it that tolerantly. A poor black neighborhood began just the other side of the tracks.

The big trouble, however, was that Edward could not maintain the sobriety of his courtship in everyday life. Although he wanted to play the role of husband, father, and wage earner, Edward also saw himself as a two-fisted, hard-drinking writer of the Hemingway mold. It would not be long after the remarriage that drinking cost him his job at the *Star-Telegram*.

Anne and Edward had a terrible row as early as Thanksgiving. Edward insisted on her cooking fried oysters for Thanksgiving dinner, while Anne wanted to prepare the traditional turkey, or at least a chicken. On another occasion, he came home drunk, and thirteen-year-old Dick Edward, whom he had taught to box, punched his father several times, breaking his dental plate and knocking him down.

By the end of the third month of their third try at marriage, Anne knew it was a failure. Yet because of their love, because of the children, because of the illogical way in which humans tend to muddle forward, Edward and Anne remained together.

If not thrilled, Edward was at least sobered by the premiere in Fort Worth of the film version of *Thieves Like Us*, which had been produced at RKO two years earlier, back in 1948, by John Houseman, with Nicholas Ray directing. But since the social conditions of the thirties had been swept away by the forties, the suggestion of social commentary in the original title was expunged by a nervous RKO, which renamed it *They Live by Night*.

Starring Farley Granger and Cathy O'Donnell as the lovers, Jay C. Flippin and Howard Da Silva as the other bandits, *They Live by Night* had reaped excellent reviews in 1948 pre-screenings. Then Howard Hughes bought RKO, shuffled management, and kept the film in the can for two years. When it was released in 1950, few publications wanted to review it again, although the *New York Times* did conscientiously state that "the story told with pictorial sincerity and emotional thrust, derives its distinction from good realistic production and sharp direction by Nicholas Ray." Houseman had picked Ray to make the story because Ray was familiar with the Southwest of the thirties and because he had worked with Texas ballad collectors John A. and Alan Lomax in their documentation of Southern folk music. The *Times* further commented on the way Ray's "sensitive juxtaposing of his actors against highways, tourist camps and bleak motels made for a vivid comprehension of an intimate personal drama in hopeless flight." Thirty-five years later, the redoubtable Houseman would say of *They Live by Night* that "it has always been one of my favorites." But without reviews in 1950, it was doomed to play mostly as the bottom half of double bills.

Anne arrived at the Fort Worth premiere excited; this story, after all, contained a lot of herself. Edward was unmoved. Newspapers interviewed him. A paperback edition of *Thieves,* under the still different title of *Your Red Wagon* (from a song in the film sung by Marie Wilson), had popped up on drugstore racks and in newsstands. The Fort Worth premiere itself was ho-hum compared with the Roman circuses at Grauman's Chinese. The thirties were over, and the five hundred bucks Anderson had gotten for his rights was long gone.

There were these interludes of sobriety, but always he returned to drinking. Finally, in the little house on Cannon, Anderson received the last, terrible seal of the serious alcoholic — delirium tremens, the "DT's." At the same time one of the children had pneumonia. Snatching occasional moments to dose the coughing child in the next room, Anne spent an afternoon pleasing Edward by running to step on red and green things that were not really creeping on the floor but inside Edward's skull. Then Edward saw and felt rats gnawing at his chest. Anne desperately sent for a doctor; physicians still made house calls in 1950. The doctor injected paraldehyde to ease Edward's wide-awake nightmare.

"If I ever get them well," Anne told herself, "I'll get out of this." She did. Before their third marriage was a year old, Anne departed to find new quarters for herself and the children. When she left, Edward burst into tears. He said, "Helen, can't you stop her? She's leaving me!" Leaving for good and all.

Anne moved the children out and got two jobs in Fort Worth to support them: days selling cosmetics in a pharmacy, nights cleaning the Tarrant County Courthouse.

Striking out west, Edward took a job on the desk of the *Avalanche-Journal* in Lubbock, a city of seventy-two thousand on the flat, dry High Plains.

The death throes of the marriage had been particularly hard on the Anderson children. Dick Edward, who had always felt somewhat overlooked by his dad, was associating with street gangs and showing an inclination to self-destruction. Helen, Edward's favorite but also quite attached to her mother, was torn. Although only fifteen, Helen used a time-sanctioned escape hatch: marriage. She had been dating a young Air Force staff sergeant named Anthony P. Gavio. Gavio proposed, and Helen said yes.

Tony Gavio, an honorable man with a strong sense of what was proper, went to Lubbock to get the consent of Helen's father. Edward at first would not be pleased to see his favorite child a bride in her early teens. Still, Gavio was a good man. Well, why not? One of Edward's colleagues on the *Avalanche-Journal* arranged for a ceremony at his own Lutheran Church of the Good Shepherd. Anne drove to Lubbock for the ceremony, and was unable to resist dating Edward afterwards. Helen and Tony's marriage worked out well. "I knew security when I saw it," Helen would say thirty-four years later; "it has been a stable and financially secure marriage."

Returning to Dallas, Edward hit up Frank King for a job at the Associated Press. King, silver-haired and mustached, had been the AP's Texas bureau chief since 1937 and was one of the nation's most respected journalists. A 1917 graduate of the University of Missouri, King had roved the world to cover the Russian Revolution, Bobby Jones's golfing grand slam, and the abdication of Edward VIII for the love of Wallis Simpson.

King sized up Anderson as an able journalist and a talented writer, though he also knew that Edward had tippled his way off the *Star-Telegram* staff. He told Anderson that he would hire him, but that if he had to fire him for drinking, he would see him blacklisted so that Anderson could never work on another major metropolitan daily. Anderson took the job, yet he could not resist alcohol. King canned him.

Perhaps the East Coast was a better place for a writer than the West. Edward went back to New York. When he got there, he went to work

Helen Anderson and Anthony Gavio's wedding at Lubbock in 1950.
Anne and Edward are at right.

on a small underground newspaper in Greenwich Village. There his plain, pugnacious writing got him into trouble. The details of his troubles there are a mystery but, like Acel Stecker in *Hungry Men,* Anderson had to leave New York suddenly.

For both Edward and his loved ones, the months and even years that followed seemed almost hallucinatory. Now in his early forties, Edward slid back toward the hobo wanderings of his twenties. He boozed, he charmed pretty women, he worked a little, and when problems caught up with him, he moved on and left them. Without a car of his own, Edward would manage to travel a hundred or so miles down the road to new bars, new girls, and eventually new problems. Perhaps he sometimes thought of Jimmie Rodgers' 1929 song about being unable to give up his rough and rowdy ways, about those railroad trains always calling him. Anderson's family would hear of him in one town, lose track of him for a time, and then learn he was someplace else. When Sergeant Gavio was transferred from Washington State to Richmond, Virginia, Helen and Tony stopped on their eastward move to visit Edward in Little Rock, Arkansas, where he was working on the newspaper. He introduced his daughter to an artist-photographer who was his current girlfriend, and the friend shot a portrait of Helen.

Edward worked for a time at the newspaper in Newport News, Virginia, and then moved on to work at a paper in Richmond. There he moved in with a Canadian woman named Myrtle who ran a rooming house in a typical, stately old Southern mansion. Edward introduced Myrtle to Helen as his wife. Helen visited the rooming house, which she found "filled with Runyonesque characters," including an American Indian in his eighties who stood more than six feet tall and insisted on demonstrating his physical prowess with high kicks. To Helen, Myrtle seemed bewildered by Edward and their ménage was already breaking up when Helen and Tony arrived in town. Edward, however, was delighted to be back in the same town with his favorite child, and even took Helen dancing once.

When he separated from Myrtle, Anderson moved in with the Gavios, even though their quarters, part of a converted barracks, had only one bedroom. He was trying again (without much success) to reshape his destructive habits; he had begun to attend Alcoholics Anonymous meetings. He still chain-smoked. The Gavios could ill afford luxuries, but Tony, who genuinely liked his father-in-law, bought Edward a carton of cigarettes. The family preserved their food in an old-fashioned icebox, and when the iceman came to deliver, Edward impulsively decided to quit smoking and gave the entire carton of cigarettes to the iceman. Edward couldn't quit, and Tony had to buy him more cigarettes. Despite AA, he couldn't quit drinking either.

"You've got to do something," said the daughter.

"What should I do, kill myself?" asked the father.

Sometimes, terribly blue, he played a mournful "I Ain't Got Nobody" on the harmonica.

Meanwhile, Anne was overworked and underfinanced as a drugstore clerk moonlighting as a janitoress, so she went out to Convair to take a test qualifying her for secretarial work. The tester advised her to train instead for a job in drafting. She enrolled in drafting classes at night and eventually went to work at Convair.

Dick Edward had begun to have serious psychological difficulties about 1950, and when Anne found a psychiatrist in Wichita Falls who seemed to help, she moved there in 1952 and found a job in drafting with Texaco. In that male-dominated profession, Anne got on well with her associates and their wives; they called her "Andy," the nickname Edward's newsroom pals in Houston had tabbed him with in 1930.

On January 6, 1954 (exactly a week after Pearl Bates died in Los Angeles), Edward became a grandfather. Tony and Helen Gavio in Richmond named their new daughter Polly Anne.

In Brownsville, a tough Texas border town of thirty-six thousand that liked to think of itself as a vacation spot, Edward got a job on the *Herald*. He then met Lupe, an attractive Mexican national. She knew almost no English, but Edward could make himself understood in Tex-Mex, and he settled down to married life with her in 1954, adopting her four-year-old son, Gerardo. A visitor to their home noted that Lupe did not drink or smoke, that she dressed modestly and wore little or no jewelry. She was not tall, and often wore her hair pulled back in a tight bun. She walked briskly, all efficiency.

Lupe, whose formal name was Evarista, gave stability to Edward's eccentric life. Maybe too much stability for Edward's taste. He drifted on to El Paso in late 1955, got a job on the *Herald-Post,* and wrote his daughter that he was thinking about divorcing Lupe. However, Lupe followed him to El Paso with the news that she was pregnant. Edward was touched.

They resumed family life in an old downtown El Paso hotel. Street urchins ran up and down the rusty fire escapes, peeping in windows; they rode the building's creaking elevators up and down. Only ten days before Edward's fifty-first birthday, on June 9, 1956, Lupe gave birth to their daughter. They decided to name her Sarita for Edward's mother, Sarah Ellen Anderson.

At the *El Paso Herald-Post* Edward worked with Chester Seltzer, another fiction writer. Seltzer was married to the former Amada Muro of Chihuahua City, Mexico, and he wrote some of his best fiction under the pen name Amado Muro. A man who had done his own share of hoboing on freights and working his passage afloat, Seltzer had read and admired Anderson's work. He would even pay Anderson the subtle compliment of entitling one Amado Muro story "Hungry Men," a story that would be published in the spring, 1967, number of the *Arizona Quarterly*. Anderson visited in the Seltzer home; the two men talked together, drank together, viewed the sights of Juárez together. When Edward shook the dust of El Paso from his feet, however, he treated Seltzer as he had J. Frank Dobie, John Knox, Dorothy Parker, Gene Fowler, and others; Seltzer never heard from him again.

Lupe, lighting Edward's cigarette

About this time Anderson happened to glance into the writing of Emanuel Swedenborg, the eighteenth-century Swedish thinker who worked to marry science to religion. All his life Anderson was an adventurous and constant reader, and since meeting John H. Knox a quarter century earlier he had concentrated on meaty books. Wherever he drifted, no matter how low his fortunes or how light his luggage, Anderson took his thesaurus and his volumes of Knut Hamsun. In Los Angeles, Richmond, El Paso, or Brownsville, Anderson was a familiar sight to public librarians. He read a hundred books a year. When he encountered the writings of the mystical Swedenborg, Anderson was fascinated. He became a convert to Swedenborg's theology, filling his conversation and his writing with Swedenborg's ideas. He wrote some letters to family and friends, attempting to proselytize them. The news of his conversion would amaze John Knox when he heard it in the early 1980s. Anne Anderson would say, "I could never associate religion with that man."

As Anderson passed into his mid-fifties, he continued to be a wanderer, continued to be incapable of sitting down long in one place. In his later wanderings, however, he stayed in Texas, still covering a vast territory, but with nothing like the scope of his freight-train-riding thirties or the East Coast jaunts that followed the breakup of his third attempt at marriage with Anne. He was loosely tethered to Brownsville, where Lupe Anderson insisted on living with Gerardo and Sarita. Lupe, with no real grasp of English, was uncomfortable away from Mexico, and more comfortable with Mexican nationals than with Hispanics born and raised in the United States. She stayed put while Edward wandered.

In the thirties, John Knox and Knut Hamsun and Anne Bates had supplied a firm center to his life; in the late fifties and the sixties, God and Swedenborg and Lupe took the same roles. To the outsider, the result was not so exciting literarily or intellectually, but to Anderson himself it was wonderful, arresting his downward slide and giving him a certain philosophic calm with which to view his career.

Before the mid-1960s Anderson had rarely had contact with his old life, except on those occasions he impulsively sent a dollar bill to Chiquita Gavio, his granddaughter, or the yearly five dollars he sent to her for her "Christmas fund." In 1961 Anderson's second granddaughter, Gina Marie Gavio, was born in Montgomery, Alabama.

Sometimes Anderson worked, sometimes he went jobless, as much as six or seven months at a whack. In such straits, Edward and Lupe, Gerardo and Sarita got money from Edward's family in Dallas.

A young student from Texas Tech named Dwight Fullingham was working in the summer of 1964 for the E. J. Storm Printing Company in Dallas, where Anderson was working as a proofreader. Learning that Fullingham was an English major, Edward mentioned his own novels, but referred to his literary career as a "flash in the pan." He didn't even have copies of his books to show the young man. On his day off, Fullingham went to the Dallas Public Library to look for *Hungry Men* and *Thieves Like Us*. No copies there. Instead he found Anderson working at a round oak library table covered with manuscript pages. Away from the print shop with its galley proofs of *Texas Quarterhorse Journal* and *Journal of Petroleum Engineering,* Anderson confided that he wanted to find a young evangelist for whom he could write sermons and promotional materials. Anderson felt that Billy Graham was largely a creation of the Hearst newspapers and that he could perform much the same trick with someone else.

As Anderson's interest in writing fiction dimmed, his interest in religion and religion's healing powers grew. In October of 1964, Anderson was working the graveyard shift from 11:00 P.M. to 7:00 A.M. as night clerk for the Cliffton Hotel in Dallas. It gave him lots of time for reading. He wrote his daughter Helen:

> . . . I have been doing a lot of research, medical, and it may be I will come up with a book in due time on the subject of diseases such as cancer, which Holy scripture describes as leprosy. . . .
>
> It's also my discovery, singular as far as I know, that the United States is unprecedented perhaps, since the Egyptians, in the worship of "graven images," automobiles, that is. Their adoration of the scarab (beatle) is historic and it is not accidental, I hold, that the most popular car in the world today is the Volkswagon, known also, as the "beatle." . . .
>
> All my thinking stems from the doctrine of Emmanuel Swedenborg, as you must well know, the greatest scientist of his day, who, at 50, discarded "science" as so much trash to pursue what he recognized to be genuinely valuable—the study of the Word.

In the remaining years of his life, Anderson would write a great deal in this tenor.

By December of that year Anderson had "rejoined the newspaper gang," going to work on the *Daily Sun* at Kermit, an oil town with a population of eight thousand. In another letter to Helen he approved of the conversion of his younger son to Lutheranism, "giving up those hypocritical Baptists," and expressing the hope he would eventually find genuine Christianity in Swedenborgianism. He was at work on a book that would expose the clergy ("What an adulterous lot the whole bunch are") with a first chapter entitled "Golden Emerods." Anderson's new religious fervor did not express itself in church attendance, and he was delighted to find the writings of another Scandinavian thinker, Søren Kierkegaard, advising worshipers not to attend church.

Small towns are perhaps more tolerant of radical opinion than *Main Street* author Sinclair Lewis would have us believe. Kermit residents would have viewed Anderson as another harmless crank, shrugged their shoulders, and enjoyed his newspaper skills. In Kermit, Anderson got acquainted with a forty-year-old minister of the Disciples of Christ persuasion who listened with some interest to Anderson's obviously sincere religious opinions. The minister at first said, "You write the sermons and I'll preach them." To Anderson he would look momentarily like the long-sought purveyor of Swedenborgian truth. Hearing a bit further into the matter, however, the minister backed off.

From Kermit, Anderson slid on to work at Alice. Then a hard year of unemployment with Lupe and the children at Brownsville followed. Anderson considered this year, during which he applied himself to Swedenborg's texts, as "preparation for a bigger deal."

16. Swedenborg, Brownsville, and -30-

Shortly before her son's sixty-first birthday, Ellen Anderson, living in Dallas, received a letter from Edward.

Dear Mama:

Guess you've been wondering about your favorite son?

This finds me in my second week [as] the editor of the *Cuero Record*. I started you the paper yesterday mainly because I'm writing a column for it.

I can see now that my leaving Kermit and Alice were "blessings in disguise." Yes, as my young preacher comrade says: "The Lord is being good to us."

The publisher here, Jack Howerton, my senior by a few years, is the kind of man I like. He started me at $110 and, yesterday, he told me: "I'll raise you $10 a week in two months; $10 more a week in two months after that until you have been here six months—then it will be $140 a week. That will be my top."

More than that: Mr. Howerton has offered to put Gerardo to work learning the printing trade. So I am going to send for him immediately.

More: there is no *ropa usada* store here (second hand dresses) and I'm going to put Lupe and Sarita in business!

More: the town is crying for "fry cooks" and I'm going to bring up here Benito and his family, wife and baby.

More: My young preacher friend has now his license to preach in all Baptist churches (he was licensed only last week) and I'm planning on setting up our headquarters here in Cuero. We intend to publish a tabloid and booklets—in time—books.

This German lad is going to move to Cuero also. He wants to come right on, but I've told him to wait until I get a house and all.

But I want to tell you that all this good fortune comes after only the utmost privation we endured in Brownsville. I felt like several times of writing you-all and telling you how hard up we were, but I had asked you for so much help in the past, I just put it off. But poor Lupe literally made the alleys behind the food stores in Brownsville to get vegetables and fruits thrown out. I saw those poor kids, Sara and Gerardo, come in from school day after day with nothing but rice and beans to eat and tortillas.

I was counting on getting on jobless employment (my claim was for $550 at $37 a week) but the Alice paper protested and stopped me. I appealed and was hitch-hiking to Austin to protest in person when I had a "hunch" to stop here in Cuero, although rides would have taken me on to San Antonio, etc.—and sure enough, they needed a man—just like yours truly!

I'm everything editorially here—editor, columnist, photographer.

But it was tough those months there in Brownsville. But I never stopped working and wrote 14 messages for [my preacher]. He addressed a convention of preachers at Freer, Texas, last month and he wrote and said:

"Those preachers really slumped down in their seats. Then their eyes would bulge out. They never heard such preaching. And after it was over, they slunk out, but some of the laymen came to me and said: 'You told the truth.'"

So you can see my lad is going to town. And that of course is the work I've been preparing to do now for so many years.

Besides the booklets I prepared in Brownsville, I just about wound up the first draft of my book which is going to expose so much in this country including the doctor racket. (I'm sorry Leon [Hodges] didn't acknowledge at least my offer, for it could have done him good. Scripture says you have done your duty when you have warned people, but to keep your mouth shut is to participate in the sins of the others.)

My greatest defect is my arrogance. I know I am better informed than most people but I owe that to Divine Providence and it is of no doing on my own part. I always have to repeat the prayer: "Lead me not into temptation . . ."

I get so impatient with ignorant people, particularly those educators who make $25,000 or so a year and up. . . . And these butchers who call themselves "doctors" and these preachers who call themselves "Christians."

They are inviting disaster. Dallas, for example, if I can calculate the least bit, is going to be erased. I hope you-all are out of there before the storm hits.

Yes, we went around in Brownsville for weeks and weeks—not a nickel—rent two months past due, etc., and sold about all that people could buy including the TV.

But it looks like we're going to go have smoother riding now.

Edward

Thus Ellen Anderson learned that her son had taken a job—it was to be his last—with Jack Howerton's little daily in Cuero. But Gerardo did not apprentice in printing, Lupe and Sarita did not open

Edward at work on a small Texas newspaper

a *ropa usada* store in Cuero, Benito (another son of Lupe's) did not move to Cuero as a fry cook. As for the Baptist preacher, an aspiring evangelist only twenty-two years old ("I am going to direct his crusade," Anderson wrote Helen, adding that along with the tabloid and tracts he hoped to publish "finally . . . my own book so many years in preparation"), that plan too eventually fell through because, Anderson believed, the young man "yellowed up on me."

Cuero, originally a German settlement, was a county seat town of

seven thousand near San Antonio. As a combination editor, columnist, photographer, and even engraver, Anderson had plenty to do filling the *Record* daily. In his byline now, he was just Ed Anderson; Andy
or Eddie sounded too youthful for a man past sixty. Edward belonged
to the respected novelist of the thirties.

Newspapering in Cuero diluted Anderson's crankiness. He had to
quit poring over his Bible so many hours a day, and he possessed the
spare change to go across the street after work for a beer or two at
the Turf. He could eat at Foodcraft Barbecue down on West Main.
Ed even went to a dance. He missed a good library. Since the family
in Brownsville had the two dogs, a Pekingese and a half-breed German shepherd, in Cuero Ed got a couple of other stray mutts, a shepherd named Lady and a mongrel with chow blood, to soothe his lone-
liness. "On these cold nights I've been letting them sleep in the extra
bed I have," Edward wrote in a 1966 letter to Helen.

Even past sixty Anderson remained lean and muscular. In the informal small-town atmosphere, Ed habitually wore knit shirts to work,
and his habit of walking kept him looking trim in them. He retained
most of his hair, grayed now, and wore glasses. He still chain-smoked.

Ed struck up an acquaintance in the Turf with Jack Rickman,
twenty-five years old, a six-footer who earlier in 1966 had completed
an Army hitch as a military policeman in Germany and was now trying to build a small service station into an oil-company dealership.
Rickman had read widely, and the two men found much to talk about.
Rickman found Anderson full of curious theories, some of them drawn
from a radical religious weekly newspaper published in Arkansas. Anderson told him that Zionism was a cover for the struggle to control
Palestine because of its potash deposits which he said held the key
to world agriculture. He told Rickman of his belief that Billy Graham
was just an actor under the wing of the Hearst newspapers and that
the United States would eventually come to a crisis that would force
the nation to ask Charles Lindbergh to lead it. He seriously advised
Rickman to follow Lindbergh without question.

Because he had to start work on the Cuero newspaper early every
morning, Anderson disliked covering night meetings. He talked Howerton into hiring Rickman for that chore.

In the fall Hugh Benbow established a training camp near Cuero
to get his fighter, Cleveland ("Big Cat") Williams, in shape for his
November 14 fight with Cassius Clay for the heavyweight champion-

ship of the world. Rickman did a feature on Williams, who had apparently recovered fully from the .357 Magnum bullet he took in the belly during a dispute two years earlier with a Texas state trooper. The young reporter then became Williams's press agent. On occasion Rickman picked up Anderson at his house on South Esplanade, and together they went to watch Big Cat train. But when the fateful night came, 35,460 fans in the Astrodome watched Clay stop Williams cold at the end of the second round. Rickman's career kept going, however, and he eventually became features editor for the *Houston Chronicle.*

Helen Gavio's letters kept her father informed about his first family, and when one of them distinguished himself, Edward commented that he was proud but hoped "he doesn't prove to be a flash in the pan like I was."

In 1967 Anderson's son Dick Edward died in Baltimore. A rebel after his parents' 1950 divorce, often in psychiatric therapy, Dick Edward served a hitch in the Army, and after his discharge he was often out of contact with his family for long periods of time. He went to prison for robbing another criminal, and after his parole, he was found in his apartment with his throat slashed. The police ruled the death a suicide, although circumstantial evidence suggested that it could have been a professional murder.

When he reached sixty-two in June of 1967, Ed Anderson gave his final "-30-" (the reporter's way of marking the end of a story), retired from the *Cuero Record* (his fifty-second newspaper), and returned to Brownsville to settle with Lupe and the kids. Now he planned to scrape by on his fifteen hundred a year from Social Security and finish *O Man, Know Thyself!,* his Swedenborg book.

Stomach problems, however, soon began to plague Anderson, but he was slow to seek medical attention. He would derive satisfaction from his own brand of Swedenborgianism—his belief that he need only reform morally to regain his health—without surrendering cash he didn't have to physicians who did, like his brother-in-law Leon Hodges. Anderson the broke writer had had to accept financial assistance from the kindly, soft-spoken doctor frequently over the years, but now Anderson the Swedenborgian could laugh at Dr. Leon and his profession.

Then in late September of 1967 came Hurricane Beulah. The great storm rode into Brownsville on winds of 160 miles per hour, accom-

panied by thirty inches of rain along the Texas and Mexican coast-
lines. In the United States, Beulah battered a rough triangle from the
Gulf of Mexico above Victoria 360 miles west to Del Rio and 200 miles
south to Port Isabel. It killed eleven Texans. In nearby Harlingen,
where Anderson had also worked on the newspaper, streets and homes
were flooded when the Rio Grande crested ten feet above flood level,
bursting dams and levees. Brownsville was less affected, although the
Andersons were without water or electricity for a couple of days. On
September 24 Anderson wrote his mother that "the night of the big
blow no one slept, not even the children. Transformers blew out nearby
with big reports and that was alarming. Big trees were uprooted all
around us, but we did not so much as get a window blown out. Lupe
had boarded up all of them." Just before Beulah hit, Anderson's old
vagabond dog, Rusti, straggled in; he stayed five days, until the emer-
gency was over, and wandered off again.

Through sickness and storm, Anderson continued to read widely
and recommended two volumes he had just finished to his elder daughter: Henri Troyat's *Tolstoy* and William Gibson's *A Mass for the Dead*. He
continued to make slurs about physicians, educators, Jews, and ministers of organized churches. He wrote of his admiration for Robert
Kennedy and Helen Keller. It was a curious mixed bag of opinions.

He finished a rough draft of *O Man, Know Thyself!* His chapter
headings, with their references to the King James Bible, hint at the
book's content:

1. Is the Common Cold a Mystery? No!
2. Stripes for a Fool's Belly
3. Our Guiding Reins: the Kidneys
4. Golden Hemorrhoids & Mice
5. America: Land of Graven Images
6. There Is a Famine in the Land (of truth)
7. The Way of the Transgressors Is Hard (hardened arteries, heart attacks)
8. The Leprosies: Cancer, Death's First-born
9. Lot's Wives (the rheumatic and arthritic)
10. Physician, Heal Thyself (Doctors die at the age of 57 and of the *sword* (heart attacks) and leprosy as Freud)
11. We Are Our Own Executioners. (Nearly all men and women commit suicide, if not in gross, then in subtle forms)

12. "Dogs, They Cannot Bark" (our clergy) from Isaiah

13. The Demon possessed (our insane)

14. O Man, Know Thyself! (There is no more difficult a thing than to "see" our defects (vices) according to Thales, one of the wisest men of ancient Greece.)

By 1969 Anderson was trying to interest the Swedenborg Foundation in his book. He needed a typewriter, however, to work on it, and it looked as though he might have to take a job on a newspaper again to get enough money for one. He happened to step into the Pilot, a beer joint where newsmen congregated, one Saturday morning and mention his dilemma to Al, a little Irishman whom Anderson considered the sharpest newsman in the Valley.

"How much is a typewriter?" asked Al.

"Oh, two hundred bucks," said Anderson.

Al wrote out a check.

"It's a gift if you don't go back on a newspaper," said Al.

Anderson, who had already arranged to return to the Brownsville newspaper staff the following Monday, considered himself spared by "Providential Care." So he settled down in March of 1969 to polish his book, estimating that he would have it ready within six months to offer to publishers.

His restless, wandering days had come to an end. His old dog Rusti had also wearied of wandering and came home for good to the housing project where Edward and Lupe lived with their son and daughter. Anderson enjoyed the visits of Lupe's children and grandchildren. Brownsville now fit him like a pair of comfortable old shoes, and after he thumped his new typewriter until he was tired, Anderson would wander into familiar downtown Brownsville, having coffee with his friend Martin Rutledge at the little hole-in-the-wall hamburger place Rutledge's family had operated since the 1920s, or rubbing elbows with fellow journalists at the Pilot.

And yet there were problems. Anderson sent out manuscripts to the editors of small religious publications, and he needed all his biblical philosophy when they came right back. His clipped, matter-of-fact style that had fitted his proletarian novels so well was ill-suited to the subtle issues of theology, but Anderson seemed unaware of that. He blamed his continuing stomach problems on his anxiety over the fact that his discoveries about the moral roots of illness would not find their way into print. The noise of the housing project irritated him, so the Andersons moved to an "old house which must be more than a century old" at 105 East Washington Street, in a quiet neighborhood. The rundown house had a gallery-type porch in front, big fireplaces, banana and fig trees in the yard, "and space still for a vegetable garden if we choose."

As summer faded toward fall, Ed puttered around the East Washington house, which he and Lupe temporarily shared only with Sarita. Gerardo, who had come to be called "Jerry," was working as a *winchero* on a Gulf shrimping boat. (Anderson had watched his stepson's high-school career with pride as Jerry played on the football team and advanced to sergeant in the school's ROTC unit.) Ed began to have symptoms of heart trouble, but Lupe and Sarita had some difficulty persuading him to go to a doctor. When the heart attack came in late August, he entered Mercy Hospital.

Down the long hospital corridor, smelling of soap and disinfectant and the other faint odors of disease and medicine, Anderson's wife and his thirteen-year-old daughter came to visit him. When they found him in the unadorned hospital room, resting between the crisp white hospital sheets, he looked strangely quiet for a man who had moved around so much all his life. They talked quietly. When the visit was over, his last words were to ask if Lupe had fed old Rusti.

Anderson died of myocardial infarction on September 5, 1969.

A long way from the thirties, a long way from Houston and Europe, from Abilene and New York, from New Orleans and Kerrville, from Denver and Hollywood, Edward E. Anderson was buried in Buena Vista Burial Park at Brownsville. His headstone is engraved with his name, birth and death dates, and a small open book with a pen lying across its pages.

But Edward Anderson also left behind two strong, good novels. Despite his lack of a literary advocate, such as Scott Fitzgerald had in Edmund Wilson, *Hungry Men* and *Thieves Like Us* continue to hold a place as minor classics in the stream of American literature. Writing in 1954 to his British publisher, Raymond Chandler, author of *Farewell My Lovely* and a half dozen other hard-boiled crime classics, mentioned "Edward Anderson who long ago wrote a book called *Thieves Like Us,* one of the best crook stories ever written."

A second film version of *Thieves Like Us,* this time released under the same title as the novel, appeared in 1974. The film was produced by Jerry Bick and directed by Robert Altman, with Keith Carradine in the role of Bowie and Shelley Duvall as Keechie. The principal setting was shifted from Texas to Mississippi. Pauline Kael, paying tribute to Anderson as "a considerable writer," called it Altman's closest approach to a flawless film. At the same time, many readers discovered the novel when it reappeared as a mass market paperback.

Hungry Men was republished in 1985 by Penguin Books with an unsigned introduction written by Gerald Howard, Penguin senior editor. Among the many favorable reviews were those in the *Saturday Review* by Susan Mernit and the *Christian Science Monitor* by James Kaufmann, who said the novel belonged on the same shelf with *The Grapes of Wrath, Let Us Now Praise Famous Men,* and Studs Terkel's *Hard Times.* Becoming acquainted with the book through this 1985 edition, Anne Banks, Bill Moyers, and Larry L. King praised it. Irving Howe called it "a strong piece of fiction about bottom-dog America" captured in prose "unsentimental, sharply written, packed with keen vignettes." A French edition of *Hungry Men* was also in print in the 1980s.

Arbor House published a new edition of *Thieves Like Us* in the spring of 1987.

A half century after they met, his friend John Knox mused on Eddie's career:

> He was like a greenhorn who had a few old golf clubs and decided to become a champ. So there he was, out there on the golf course, having knocked a few balls around and that's all. But what happened? Right off he hit a hole-in-one, won a fairly prestigious prize.
>
> Well, accidents will happen, eh? So now he sat down and wrote a second book. This was the tough one. Writers have gone nuts and blown their brains out at this hurdle. But he wrote this book, and it ended up having two movies made out of it. Tell me, how many writers have ever done that?

Anderson was gifted and intelligent, but his gift proved good only for one specific time and place. He coupled his style, plain and low-keyed, to "poor-folks" stories—just the mix for the leftish thirties. There was no better time to produce a proletarian novel than the year of the great communist-inspired Writers Congresses in New York and Paris.

When the thirties were finished, his gifts no longer suited. There had been a subtle shift in the intellectual floor beneath him, like the settling of the foundations of a house. Nothing dramatic, and yet one morning a door would no longer fit its cockeyed frame, a window would no longer come up in its sash. Other proletarian novelists — Robert Cantwell, Jack Conroy, Mike Gold, and Henry Roth come to mind — seem to have had similar problems adjusting. At any rate, Anderson could not adjust any better than his printer father had been able to learn the newfangled Linotype machines.

When the thirties were over, the spell broken, the important friendships killed by quarrel or neglect, Anderson was intelligent enough to realize it, and regret it. Intelligence carries its cost. He drank and drank, and his life with Anne and their children was wrecked.

Coming in his early maturity as they did, Anderson's books led everyone to expect even greater achievements of him. If Anderson had written his two little masterpieces toward the end of his life, they would seem a culmination rather than an anticlimax. As time passes the importance of the sequence dims. The fact remains: Edward Anderson left behind two strong, good novels.

Sources

Edward E. Anderson kept no journal and seldom wrote letters during his most creative years. I have pieced together his story mostly by talking, or exchanging letters, with a large number of persons who knew him, who knew his friends, or knew his times.

Anne Bates Anderson, Edward's wife during the thirties and forties, was most helpful, and without her this book could not have been written. John H. Knox, Helen Anderson Gavio, Imogene Anderson Hodges, and Ellen Sexton Anderson also told me things that only they could tell.

Among the many others who gave me invaluable information were Dorothy Anderson, Gerardo Anderson, Harold ("Prexy") Anderson, Gay Balch, Caroline Couch Blair, Brandt and Brandt literary agency, Roy Campbell, Oscar del Castillo, Olen Clements, Bob Compton, Horace Condley, Courtney Cowan, Jean Stapleton Curtis, Martha A. Dobie, Don Duncan, Maureen Eastus, Victor Emanuel, Valerie (Melba Newton) Edinger, Sybil (Mrs. Francis) Finberg, Albert Gold, Alfonso Gonzales, John Graves, A.C. Greene, Elbert Hall, Everett Haney, Jay Harris, Mrs. Jack Howerton, Russell Howerton, Elsie Lorene (Mrs. John H.) Knox, John K. Knox, Amber Scott Long, Mrs. Claud ("Tid") McAden, Marvin Miller, W. O. Norman, Jewell Posey, Tom Reed, Jack Rickman, Elzie Robbins, Meta Rosenberg, Martin Rutledge, Forrest Saltzer, Chuck Schwanitz, Amada (Mrs. Charles) Seltzer, Fannie Dobie Stanford, Dorothy Stowe, Macon Sumerlin, Naomi Taniguchi, Lorene Stutts Heitchew Tessmer, Dorris Tull, Barbara Bentley Wade, Ruth Knox Wall, Ed N. Wishcamper, and Clay Zachry, Jr.

Among those helping with research or offering suggestions were Frank Beesley, Shay W. Bennett, Lindsay A. Davies, Foster Foreman,

Paul Foreman, Patricia A. Garcia, Philippe Garnier, Leon Hale, Gerald Howard, William H. Hunt, Paul Jungmeyer, Julian Long, James ("Jay") Rushing, Jane Gilmore Rushing, Allison Sanders, Joyce Spencer Sandlin, Mildred Shirley, Joseph D. Stamey, Susan Throckmorton, Frances Vaughn, and Thomas Zigal.

CHAPTER 1. The description of Edward Anderson is chiefly from the memory of Anne Anderson. Melba Newton, now known as Valerie Edinger, told me about Edward's proposal of marriage to her, as did Anne Anderson and Imogene Hodges. Prexy Anderson recalled Edward's boast about working on twenty-six newspapers. Imogene Hodges recalled Edward's one prizefight and his trip to Europe.

CHAPTER 2. The description of Abilene owes much to bankers Elzie Robbins, W. O. Norman, and Everett Haney. Ellen Anderson and Imogene Hodges told me about the Anderson family to which Edward returned. Roy Campbell took me through the house where the Andersons lived. Maureen Eastus described the *Reporter-News* offices. Barbara Wade and Ed Wishcamper recalled the career and personality of Max Bentley. Amber Long related the incident involving M. T. Scott. John H. Knox recalled his early impressions of Edward.

CHAPTER 3. A. C. Greene remembered Maude E. Cole, the Carnegie Library, and Mrs. Cole's tiff with the library board. John H. Knox recalled the Abilene writers of the day, with additional information on Files Bledsoe from Elbert Hall and Tom Reed; on Houston Heitchew from Horace Condley, Russell Howerton, Lorene Tessmer, and Ed Wishcamper; on Francis Finberg from Sybil Finberg. Imogene Hodges again recalled the incidents from Edward's early years. Anne Anderson told me the story that Edward would frequently relate when he was quite drunk. John H. Knox recalled that Edward's first sale to the pulps was "The Little Spic."

CHAPTER 4. John H. Knox recalled taking Edward to a small town nearby to begin his odyssey, but couldn't recall the town's name. The details of a typical thirties cafe are from my own memory. Knox also discussed Anderson's turn to serious fiction, his reading, and his admiration of Knut Hamsun.

CHAPTER 5. Some of the information on Stanley Walker and his Abilene connection is from Tid McAden. Maureen Eastus and others discussed John H. Knox at this period. Anne Anderson and Ruth Wall talked of Mabel Bishop Kimble. Edward's return, the writing of the novel, and the choice of title were from Knox.

CHAPTER 6. The memory of Anne Anderson is the source of almost all of this: the first encounters with Edward, the courtship, the wedding. Jewell Posey added some touches about Polly Anne Bates, the First Methodist Church, and its minister. Imogene Hodges recalled the Anderson family reaction to Polly Anne and said that Max Bentley got Edward the job with William McCraw.

CHAPTER 7. Anne Anderson is the principal source on their honeymoon, their New Orleans days, and the birth of Helen. Knox recalled that Edward had told him about the falling out with the New Orleans police. Albert Gold gave me information on Karl Sherman. John Graves recalled the character of Martha Foley.

I got the story of the mistaken identity of Prexy Anderson from him and from a clipping of his column in Anne Anderson's scrapbook.

CHAPTER 8. Anne Anderson is the major source on the genesis of the second novel and events at Huntsville and Kerrville. Imogene Hodges told me some things about Roy Johnson. Forrest Saltzer discussed J. Frank Dobie and showed me the place where Edward, Anne, and Helen lived. Martha Dobie told me a great deal about her brother, J. Frank Dobie. John Knox told me about the events involving himself.

CHAPTER 9. Anne Anderson recalled the character of Mabel Knox, the talks she witnessed between John H. Knox and Edward, life with Edward and Helen in the cabin, her own suggestions about Keechie's dialogue, and the incident of the poisoned dogs. John H. Knox recalled Edward's attitude toward Dobie, Dobie's character and actions, Edward's refusal to sell *Thieves Like Us* as a true detective serial, Edward's character, their final argument, and Edward's later remark about it to Luther Bates.

CHAPTER 10. Anne Anderson remembered the return to Abilene, the WPA Writers' Project job, the sale of the gray Ford, the move to Denver, and events there. Elsie Lorene Knox supplied details of Knox's later life, and Knox himself spoke of his later intellectual interests. Imogene Hodges recalled the relations of Anne to the E. H. Anderson family, and details of the death of E. H.

CHAPTER 11. Anne Anderson is the source of almost all the information here that is not from printed sources. Budd Schulberg recalled Anderson as a shy man, and supplied information on B. P. Schulberg's residence and the character of his parties. Anne could not recall the name of Edward's agent, but Budd Schulberg and Meta Rosenberg agreed it was almost certainly Ad Schulberg. At Anne's request, I have supplied the amnesia victim with a fictitious name.

CHAPTER 12. Although this chapter is based primarily on Anne's memory, Helen Gavio's distinct recollections of houses, scenes, and visits begin at this period. The length of Edward's employment at Warner Brothers is unclear, but this is how Anne recalled it.

CHAPTER 13. Helen Gavio recalled many details of the Anderson residences and the family good times of this period. Anne Anderson told of Edward covering Barrymore's death, his scheme for a Barrymore biography, and his anti-Semitism. Prexy Anderson recalled Edward's Barrymore obituary and Edward's anti-Semitism.

CHAPTER 14. Helen Gavio's memory was full of this period, although she naturally did not know the details of the domestic dispute and other grown-up matters that Anne Anderson recalled vividly.

CHAPTER 15. Early parts of the chapter dealing with the remarriage of Edward and Anne were recalled by Anne Anderson, as were other portions of the chapter touching on Anne's life. Helen Gavio provided information on her wedding to Tony Gavio. Imogene Hodges told of Edward's trip to New York. Helen Gavio recalled her meetings with Edward during his wanderings in the South and Southeast, and his later marriages to Myrtle and Lupe. Amada Seltzer recalled Edward's friendship with her husband.

CHAPTER 16. Alfonso Gonzales and Jack Rickman told me something of Edward in Cuero. Imogene Hodges and Gerardo Anderson recalled Edward's death in Brownsville. The opinions of Anne Banks, Bill Moyers, Larry King, and Irving Howe on *Hungry Men* are drawn from letters to Gerald Howard.

Other Sources

Abilene Reporter-News, files.
Anderson, Anne. Scrapbook.
   Three newspaper features on Edward Anderson by Melba Newton, M. L. T. (probably Michael T. Looby), and W. B. (probably Wendell Bedichek). "Poets of Texas: John H. Knox, Western Troubadour," newspaper feature by Hilton R. Greer. Newspaper feature on Dorothy McCleary. Two telegrams and a letter from Ber-

nice Baumgartern. Letter from Edward O'Brien. Reviews of *Hungry Men*. Review of Karl Sherman one-man show. Pencil portrait and caricature of Edward by Karl Sherman. "Prexy's Muse," newspaper column by Harold ("Prexy") Anderson. Titles of Edward's magazine stories clipped from tables of contents. Photographs of Edward, Anne, Dorothy Anderson, and baby Helen. Newspaper clippings on the birth of Helen, the death of E. H. Anderson, the sale of Edward's second novel, and other miscellaneous items.

Dallas Morning News, files.

Ganey, Madge Morrison. "History of Abilene Public Library," with newspaper clippings and other materials, in the administrative files of the Abilene Public Library.

Gavio, Helen. Letters from her father Edward Anderson, documents, manuscripts, photographs, and other items.

Lack, Paul, and Gerald McDaniel. "Did the Jazz Age Come to Abilene?" Paper presented at the West Texas State Historical Association meeting, March 28, 1980.

Ramsey, David. "Max Bentley." Undergraduate paper, *Abilene Reporter-News* library.

Bibliography

Allen, Frederick Lewis. *Only Yesterday: An Informal History of the Nineteen-Twenties.* New York: Harper and Brothers, 1931.

————. *Since Yesterday: The Nineteen-Thirties in America, September 3, 1929–September 3, 1939.* New York: Harper and Brothers, 1940.

Anderson, Edward. *Hungry Men.* Garden City, N.Y.: Doubleday, 1935.

————. *Thieves Like Us.* New York: Frederick A. Stokes, 1937.

Bledsoe, Thomas [Files], ed. and trans., and Guillem Colom. *Poems in Praise of Fray Junipero Serra and the Missions He Founded in California.* Palma de Mallorca: privately printed, 1969.

Chandler, Raymond. *Selected Letters.* Edited by Frank McShane. New York: Columbia University Press, 1981.

Cowley, Malcolm. *The Dream of the Golden Mountains: Remembering the 1930s.* New York: Viking, 1980.

————. *Exile's Return: A Literary Odyssey of the 1920s.* London: Bodley Head, n.d.

————. *Think Back on Us . . . : A Contemporary Chronicle of the 1930s.* Edited by Henry Dan Piper. Carbondale: Southern Illinois University Press, 1967.

Donaldson, Frances. *Edward VIII: A Biography of the Duke of Windsor.* New York: J. B. Lippincott Company, 1974.

Downs, Fane. ed. *The Future Great City of West Texas, Abilene: 1881–1981.* Abilene, Tex.: Rupert N. Richardson Press, 1981.

Duff, Katharyn, and Betty Kay Seibt. *Catclaw Country: An Informal History of Abilene in West Texas.* Burnet, Tex.: Eakin Press, 1980.

Dumont, Lou. "Shirley Ross." *Hobbies* 80, no. 5 (July, 1975): 54–55, 58–59, 128.

Faith, William Robert. *Bob Hope: A Life in Comedy.* New York: G. P. Putnam's Sons, 1982.

Finch, Christopher, and Linda Rosenkrantz. *Gone Hollywood.* Garden City, N.Y.: Doubleday, 1979.

Floan, Howard R. *William Saroyan.* New York: Twayne, 1966.

Foley, Martha. *The Story of* Story *Magazine*. New York: W. W. Norton, 1980.

Fortune, Jan I. *The True Story of Bonnie and Clyde, as Told by Bonnie's Mother and Clyde's Sister*. New York: New American Library, 1968.

Fowler, Gene. *Good Night, Sweet Prince: The Life and Times of John Barrymore*. New York: Viking, 1944.

————. *Minutes of the Last Meeting*. New York: Viking, 1954.

Fowler, Will. *The Young Man from Denver: A Candid and Affectionate Biography of Gene Fowler by His Son Will Fowler*. Garden City, N.Y.: Doubleday, 1962.

Furnas, J. C. *Great Times: An Informal Social History of the United States, 1914–1929*. New York: G. P. Putnam's Sons, 1974.

————. *Stormy Weather: Crosslights on the Nineteen-Thirties: An Informal Social History of the United States, 1929–1941*. New York: G. P. Putnam's Sons, 1977.

Goodstone, Tony. *The Pulps*. New York: Chelsea House, 1970.

Greene, A.C. *A Personal Country*. New York: Alfred A. Knopf, 1969.

————. *The Santa Claus Bank Robbery*. New York: Alfred A. Knopf, 1972.

Heide, Robert, and John Gilman. *Dime Store Dream Parade: Popular Culture, 1925–1955*. New York: E. P. Dutton, 1979.

Hope, Bob, and Bob Thomas. *The Road to Hollywood: My 40-Year Love Affair with the Movies*. Garden City, N.Y.: Doubleday, 1977.

Houseman, John. *Front and Center*. New York: Simon and Schuster, 1979.

Keats, John. *You Might as Well Live: The Life and Times of Dorothy Parker*. New York: Simon and Schuster, 1970.

Kinney, Arthur F. *Dorothy Parker*. Boston: Twayne, 1978.

Kinross, Lord. *The Windsor Years*. New York: Viking, 1967.

Kotsilibas-Davis, James. *The Barrymores: The Royal Family in Hollywood*. New York: Crown Publishers, 1981.

Lack, Paul D., Robert W. Sledge, Fane Downs, and Paul Jungmeyer. *The History of Abilene: Facts and Sources*. Abilene, Tex.: McMurry College, 1981.

Madden, David, ed. *Proletarian Writers of the Thirties*. Carbondale: Southern Illinois University Press, 1968.

Perelman, S. J. *The Last Laugh*. New York: Simon and Schuster, 1981.

Powdermaker, Hortense. *Hollywood, the Dream Factory: An Anthropologist Looks at the Movie-Makers*. Boston: Little, Brown, 1950.

Quinn, Anthony. *The Original Sin: A Self Portrait*. Boston: Little, Brown, 1972.

Robinson, Edward G., and Leonard Spigelgass. *All My Yesterdays: An Autobiography*. New York: Hawthorn Books, 1973.

Saroyan, William. *Obituaries*. Berkeley, Calif.: Creative Arts Book Company, 1979.

Schlesinger, Arthur M., Jr. *The Coming of the New Deal*. Boston: Houghton Mifflin, 1959.

————. *The Crisis of the Old Order: 1919–1933*. Boston: Houghton Mifflin, 1957.

Schulberg, Budd. *The Disenchanted*. New York: Random House, 1950.

———. *Moving Pictures: Memories of a Hollywood Prince.* New York: Stein and Day, 1981.

Shattuck, Roger. *The Innocent Eye: On Modern Literature and the Arts.* New York: Farrar, Straus, and Giroux, 1984.

Silke, James R. *Here's Looking at You, Kid: 50 Years of Fighting, Working and Dreaming at Warner Bros.* Boston: Little, Brown, 1976.

Simmons, Lee. *Assignment Huntsville: Memoirs of a Texas Prison Official.* Austin: University of Texas Press, 1957.

Smith, H. Allen. *The Life and Legends of Gene Fowler.* New York: William Morrow, 1977.

Smith, Page. *Dissenting Opinions: The Selected Essays of Page Smith.* Berkeley, Calif.: North Point Press, 1984.

Tinkle, Lon. *An American Original: The Life of J. Frank Dobie.* Boston: Little, Brown, 1978.

Van Dusen, Wilson. *The Presence of Other Worlds.* New York: William Morrow, 1977.

Vann, William H. *The Texas Institute of Letters: 1936–1966.* Austin, Tex.: Encino Press, 1967.

Walker, Stanley. *City Editor.* New York: Frederick A. Stokes, 1934.

Wilson, Edmund. *The American Earthquake.* Garden City, N.Y.: Doubleday, 1958.

———. *The Thirties: From Notebooks and Diaries of the Period.* Edited by Leon Edel. New York: Farrar, Straus, and Giroux, 1980.

———. *The Twenties: From Notebooks and Diaries of the Period.* Edited by Leon Edel. New York: Farrar, Straus, and Giroux, 1975.

Workers of the Federal Writers' Project of the Works Progress Administration. *New Orleans City Guide.* American Guide Series. Boston: Houghton Mifflin, 1938.

Workers of the Writers' Program of the Work Projects Administration. *Colorado: A Guide to the Highest State.* American Guide Series. New York: Hastings House, 1941.

Workers of the Writers' Program of the Work Projects Administration. *Los Angeles: A Guide to the City and Its Environs.* American Guide Series. New York: Hastings House, 1941.

Workers of the Writers' Program of the Work Projects Administration. *Texas: A Guide to the Lone Star State.* American Guide Series. New York: Hastings House, 1940.

Index

Rough and Rowdy Ways was composed into type on a Compugraphic digital phototypesetter in eleven point Baskerville with two points of spacing between the lines. The display type was furnished from a typewriter of the period. The book was designed by Jim Billingsley, typeset by Metricomp, Inc., printed offset by Thomson-Shore, Inc., and bound by John H. Dekker & Sons. The paper on which the book is printed bears acid-free characteristics for an effective life of at least three hundred years.

TEXAS A&M UNIVERSITY PRESS : COLLEGE STATION